FISHES OF TAIWAN AND ADJACENT WATERS

DR. WARREN E. BURGESS
DR. HERBERT R. AXELROD

1. *Balistoides niger* (Bonnaterre). The clown triggerfish is still one of the most highly prized marine aquarium fishes; juveniles under 13 cm have never been described. Photo by K.H. Choo. Taiwan.

PACIFIC MARINE
FISHES
BOOK 5
*Additional families are
covered in Book 4.
In collaboration with Dr.
Shih-chieh Shen.*

TABLE OF CONTENTS

ISBN 0-87666-127-4

FISHES OF TAIWAN AND ADJACENT WATERS

INTRODUCTION

In *Pacific Marine Fishes* Book 4 we presented the families of marine fishes which are NOT presented in this present volume. This two volume work on the fishes of Taiwan is probably the most complete review of the fishes of this area that has ever been presented and many of the fishes contained in these two books have never been photographed and published before.

In recent years, Taiwan has become more and more important as a source of aquarium fishes, both freshwater and marine. This stems from Taiwan's almost unlimited source of *Tubifex* worms, probably the best and most commonly used food for aquarium fishes. Taiwan is also the center for the manufacture of freeze-dried *Tubifex* worms, brine shrimp and other common fish foods, and the Taiwanese government is encouraging the utilization of these replenishable natural resources.

Because of the high priority placed upon the utilization of aquarium fishes as an export commodity, the Chinese government, through the Taiwan National University, has been of invaluable assistance. Dr. Shih-chieh Shen, who studied at the Smithsonian Institution as well as in Taiwan, has freely given of his time and talents in the preparation of this series of two books. He collected many of the fishes, measured and photographed them, and made the films available to us, in many cases supplying suggested identifications as well.

Many of the larger, deep-sea fishes are almost impossible to photograph, as are many of the very delicate species which lose their color and even their scales almost as soon as they are removed from the water. To properly show these fishes we've had to rely upon the excellent drawings of the famous Japanese artists Tomita, Arita and Kumada whose drawings were made available to us by Kodansha Publishing Co., Ltd., Tokyo, Japan. Many of these illustrations first appeared in the Japanese books *Japanese Fishes*, ©1971 Kodansha, and *Edible and Poisonous Fishes of the Pacific Ocean*, ©1972 Kodansha.

Book 5, the present volume, contains the families which are most familiar to one of the authors (WEB) inasmuch as he has submitted his doctoral thesis on the marine butterflyfishes of the world and is considered as being the world's authority on angelfishes and butterflyfishes. Therefore this section is quite confidently presented in terms of the proper and most up-to-date nomenclature. With several of the other groups, many experts have been consulted but as is almost always the case, different experts have differing ideas as to what a particular fish should be called. As with the previous volumes of this series which have already been reprinted, changes in nomenclature have been made to conform with acceptable American usage. There is still considerable controversy existing between Japanese, European and American ichthyologists in reference to their approach to the classification of many fishes.

Almost all of the photographs in Books 4 and 5 have never appeared in print before and while many fishes have quite a wide distribution, a careful comparison of those from Taiwan with those of distant areas highlight some very interesting and subtle differences.

As we write this Introduction, we have before us thousands of photographs for the next several volumes in this series. There is no question in our minds that the South Pacific volumes coming up will feature some of the most spectacular photographs of fishes ever taken.

Herbert R. Axelrod

Warren E. Burgess

2. *Pomacanthus imperator* (Bloch). Juvenile. Angelfishes usually are aggressive in a marine aquarium, especially if kept with members of their own species. Photo by K.H. Choo.

3. *Pomacanthus imperator* (Bloch). Sub-adult. The preopercular spine is one of the characteristics of the angelfishes. Photo by K.H. Choo.

4. *Pomacanthus imperator* (Bloch). Juvenile. Very small individuals, such as this one, are hard to find when collecting on coral reefs. Photo by Dr. Shih-chieh Shen. Chi-Lung, northeastern part of Taiwan. (50 mm standard length)

5. *Pomacanthus imperator* (Bloch). Sub-adult. A partially transformed individual makes it easy to identify the juvenile with adult patterns since portions of both can be seen. Photo by K.H. Choo. Taiwan.

6. *Pomacanthus imperator* (Bloch). The dorsal fin spines remain white throughout life, as shown in these photos. Photo by K.H. Choo. Taiwan.

7. *Pomacanthus imperator* (Bloch). A 100-gallon tank would be adequate for this size emperor angelfish. Photo by K.H. Choo. Taiwan.

8 & 9. *Pomacanthus imperator* (Bloch) (above) and *Pomacanthus semicirculatus* (Cuvier & Valenciennes) (below) juveniles. These two species are most apt to be imported for the aquarium trade. The differences between the two can easily be seen. Photos by K.H. Choo. Taiwan.

10. *Pomacanthus semicirculatus* (Cuvier and Valenciennes). Juvenile just prior to metamorphosis of the color pattern. The brownish adult background color is partially visible. Photo by K.H. Choo. Taiwan.

11. *Pomacanthus semicirculatus* (Cuvier and Valenciennes). Adult exhibiting the pointed dorsal and anal fins. Photo by Dr. Shih-chieh Shen. Chuan-fan-Shih, southern tip of Taiwan. (201.0 mm standard length)

12. *Chaetodontoplus septentrionalis* (Temminck and Schlegel). Blue-lined angelfish are best kept apart from others of their own species because of their quarrelsome nature. Photo by Dr. Shih-chieh Shen. Taiwan. (153 mm standard length)

13. *Chaetodontoplus septentrionalis* (Temminck and Schlegel). Small scales give the species of *Chaetodontoplus* a velvety appearance. Photo by K.H. Choo. Taiwan.

14. *Chaetodontoplus septentrionalis* (Temminck and Schlegel). The young of several species of *Chaetodontoplus* exhibit the yellow band through the pectoral fin. Photo by Dr. Shih-chieh Shen. Taiwan. (28.8 mm standard length).

15. *Chaetodontoplus septentrionalis* (Temminck and Schlegel). Subadult. Vegetable matter (greens) should be a part of the aquarium diet of this species. Photo by K.H. Choo. Taiwan.

16. *Chaetodontoplus duboulayi* (Gunther). Previously unrecorded from Taiwan, the scribbled angelfish attains a length of about one foot. The band through the pectoral fin base, the caudal fin, and the stripe at the base of the dorsal fin are all bright yellow. Photo by Dr. Shih-chieh Shen. Taiwan. (120 mm standard length)

17. *Chaetodontoplus personifer* (McCulloch). This is another species that apparently has been unrecorded from Taiwan until now. It was thought to occur only in Australia. Photo by Dr. Shih-chieh Shen. Taiwan. (177 mm standard length)

18. *Chaetodontoplus personifer* (McCulloch). The characteristic yellow spots on the head are more clearly seen on this specimen. Photo by Dr. Shih-chieh Shen. Taiwan. (220 mm standard length)

19. *Chaetodontoplus personifer* (McCulloch). Notice the caudal fin pattern in contrast to that of other species. Illustration by Tomita.

20. *Chaetodontoplus melanosoma* (Bleeker). Juvenile. Most individuals of this species available for sale are larger than this one and have already lost the juvenile yellow bar behind the head. Photo by Dr. Shih-chieh Shen. Kee-Lung, northern tip of Taiwan. (60 mm standard length)

21. *Euxiphipops sexstriatus* (Cuvier). Adult. This is one of the larger angelfishes and may reach a length of almost 2 feet. Photo by Dr. Shih-chieh Shen. Kee-Lung, northern tip of Taiwan. (155.6 mm standard length)

22. *Pygoplites diacanthus* (Boddaert). Adult. Not all angelfishes undergo radical color changes from juvenile to adult stage. Photo by Dr. Shih-chieh Shen. Taiwan. (233 mm standard length)

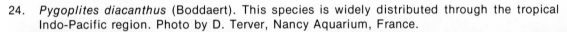

23. *Pygoplites diacanthus* (Boddaert). Juvenile. The ocellated spot is soon lost in the blue-dotted pattern of the dorsal fin. Illustration by Arita.

24. *Pygoplites diacanthus* (Boddaert). This species is widely distributed through the tropical Indo-Pacific region. Photo by D. Terver, Nancy Aquarium, France.

25. *Apolemichthys trimaculatus* (Lacepede). Adults are often available for sale and do fairly well in captivity. Large tank space is, of course, needed. Photo by Dr. Shih-chieh Shen. Taiwan. (139 mm standard length)

26. *Apolemichthys trimaculatus* (Lacepede). Adult. Angelfishes are very much at home among the corals. Once acclimated to the home aquarium, they will appear frequently in the open water. Photo by K.H. Choo. Taiwan.

27 & 28.   *Apolemichthys trimaculatus* (Lacepede). Juveniles have a prominent spot in the dorsal fin and a faintly barred pattern. Note that the upper fish lacks the characteristic black band on the anal fin. Perhaps it will appear as the fish grows. Photos by Dr. Shih-chieh Shen. Upper fish from Chi-Lung, northeastern part of Taiwan (40 mm standard length); lower fish from Kee-Lung, northern tip of Taiwan. (44.1 mm standard length)

29. *Genicanthus watanabei* (Yasuda & Tominaga). This is the adult female. The male has striping in the ventral part of the body (see PMF Book 1, p. 17). Photo by Dr. Shih-chieh Shen. Kee-Lung, northern tip of Taiwan. (84.6 mm standard length)

30. *Apolemichthys trimaculatus* (Lacepede). Notice the purplish-colored lips of this species. Photo by K.H. Choo. Taiwan.

31. *Centropyge ferrugatus* Randall and Burgess. This species has now been recorded from southern Japan to Taiwan. Perhaps its range will eventually be found to extend much further. Photo by K.H. Choo. Taiwan.

32. *Centropyge ferrugatus* Randall and Burgess. The reddish color is much more intense in these individuals. If the aquarium conditions are ideal, the fish will show off their best livery. Photo by K.H. Choo. Taiwan.

33. *Centropyge ferrugatus* Randall and Burgess. These preserved specimens were among the first of this species to be collected in Taiwan. Photo by Dr. Shih-chieh Shen. Taiwan. (upper fish 54.8 mm standard length; lower fish 68.0 mm standard length)

34. *Centropyge ferrugatus* Randall and Burgess. Although live, this individual has lost the brighter orange-red color and has assumed the lighter color of the preserved specimens. Photo by K.H. Choo. Taiwan.

35.
Centropyge heraldi Woods and Schultz. The delicate pattern of orange stripes can clearly be seen in this specimen. Photo by Dr. Shih-chieh Shen. Taiwan. (66.0 mm standard length)

36.   *Centropyge heraldi* Woods and Schultz. This species may be more common than the better known aquarium favorite, *C. flavissimus* (the lemon peel). Photo by K.H. Choo. Taiwan.

37. *Centropyge vroliki* (Bleeker). The dark area posteriorly varies in extent. Here it covers little of the body. Photo by Dr. Shih-chieh Shen. Taiwan. (74.1 mm standard length)

38. *Centropyge vroliki* (Bleeker). Here the dark area covers much more of the posterior end of the body. Photo by K.H. Choo. Taiwan.

39. *Centropyge bicolor* (Bloch). This species is one of the few in the genus which possesses an eye band. Photo by K.H. Choo. Taiwan.

40. *Centropyge bispinosus* (Gunther). The amount of orange color in this species varies widely. Here it is reduced to a small amount. Photo by K.H. Choo. Taiwan.

41. *Centropyge nox* Bleeker. The bright light used to photograph this fish caused it to look brownish rather than black. Aquarium specimens would look almost solid black. Photo by K.H. Choo. Taiwan.

42. *Centropyge tibicen* (Cuvier and Valenciennes). Note the blue line bordering the inner edge of the yellow anal fin band. Photo by K.H. Choo. Taiwan.

43. *Centropyge tibicen* (Cuvier and Valenciennes). The scales in angelfishes are ridged. These ridges can be discerned in several of the scales of this preserved specimen. Photo by Dr. Shih-chieh Shen. Taiwan. (41.2 mm standard length)

44. *Centropyge tibicen* (Cuvier and Valenciennes). The bluish spot above the pectoral fin usually is lost in the body color. Photo by Dr. Shih-chieh Shen. Ho-bi-Hou, southern tip of Taiwan. (36.3 mm standard length)

45. *Platax orbicularis* (Forskal). Young batfish, especially this species, are frequently available at stores that sell marine aquarium fishes. They are hardy and grow well. Photo by Dr. Shih-chieh Shen. Wan-Li-Tung, southern tip of Taiwan. (40.5 mm standard length)

46. *Platax orbicularis* (Forskal). Juvenile. Wide ranging Indo-Pacific species. Photo by K.H. Choo. Taiwan.

Family EPHIPPIDAE
SPADEFISHES, BATFISHES, ETC.

The spadefishes and their relatives have long been problematical to ichthyologists, and the division of these fishes into families has gone in various directions. The three groups causing the confusion are the spadefishes, batfishes, and the sicklefishes. They have been: 1) regarded as separate families Ephippidae, Platacidae, and Drepanidae; 2) combined into different assemblages of these families; or 3) grouped under a single family, the Ephippidae. At present it seems best to include all these fishes under a single family. This group is being studied by one of the authors (WEB) in hopes of straightening out some of the confusion.

One group especially is considered as excellent aquarium fishes. These are the batfishes (Platacinae), which were covered in Book 1 (p. 78). A second group, the spadefishes (Ephippinae), seems to be just as hardy under aquarium conditions, and similar problems of outgrowing their tanks may occur. The Atlantic spadefish is dark brown to blackish when young, changing to silver with black stripes with age. Bat-

47.   *Platax teira* (Forskal). Adult batfishes look very much alike and are difficult to separate. Juveniles are more distinctive and therefore more easily distinguished. Illustration by Arita.

fishes also start out brown or black and also become more silvery with age. Like the batfishes, the spadefish when young is an excellent mimic of dead leaves and other floating objects and relies on the camouflage of color and behavior for its major protection.

The Ephippinae, like other members of the family, are deep bodied, compressed fishes which are covered by moderate sized scales. The scales extend onto the soft dorsal, anal, and caudal fins. The head is deeper than long and also covered with small scales. The mouth is small and provided with bands of setiform teeth. The mouth and tooth structure are reminiscent of the angelfishes, family Pomacanthidae. No teeth are present on the palate. A single dorsal fin is present, though deeply notched, and the spinous part is composed of about ten spines. A procumbent spine precedes the dorsal fin. The membranes of the spinous dorsal fin are deeply incised. The soft dorsal and anal fins are similar in shape and about equal in size, and are placed opposite each other. Unlike some of the other members of the family, the pectoral fins are small and rounded. The pelvic fins are thoracic and provided with an axillary scaly process. Three genera have normally been placed in this subfamily, *Ephippus*, *Chaetodipterus*, and *Tripterodon*. *Tripterodon* has a weak ocular shelf compared to the other two and has often been placed in a separate family (or subfamily). In addition, its teeth are not setiform but are tricuspid and compressed. *Ephippus* may be distinguished from *Chaetodipterus* by its larger scales, prolonged, slender third to fifth dorsal fin spines, and by having the second anal spine not larger than the third. The only member of this family that reaches China is *Ephippus orbis*. It extends from Taiwan through the East Indies to the coast of Africa. It reaches a length of about 190 mm.

The Drepaninae are very similar in appearance to the Ephippinae. They can easily be distinguished by the pectoral fin however, that of the drepanids being long and falcate. Other characters that have been used for separation are the subocular

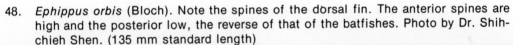

48. *Ephippus orbis* (Bloch). Note the spines of the dorsal fin. The anterior spines are high and the posterior low, the reverse of that of the batfishes. Photo by Dr. Shih-chieh Shen. (135 mm standard length)

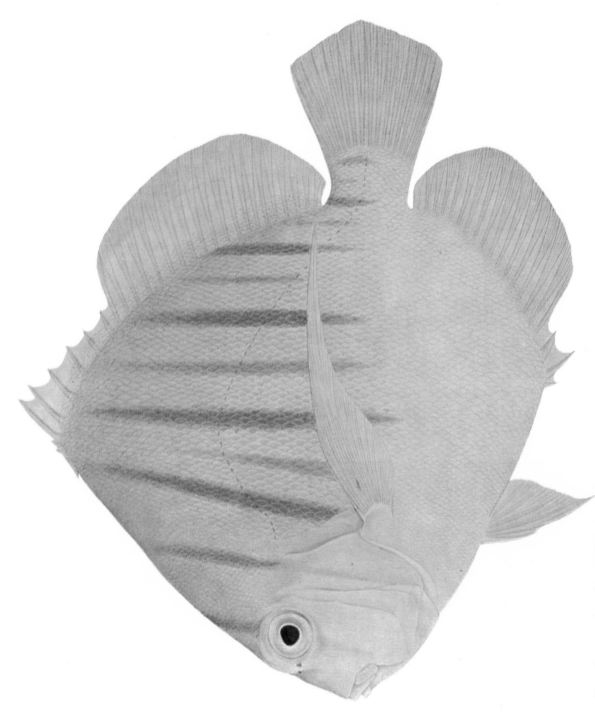

49. *Drepane longimana* (Bloch and Schneider). This species is often confused with *Drepane punctata*, but has stripes instead of rows of spots. Illustration by Arita. East and west coasts of Africa to Australia.

shelf (present in the ephippids but absent in the drepanids), the more protractile mouth of the drepanids, and the distally exposed maxillary of the drepanids (hidden in the ephippids). There are bands of setiform teeth in the jaws but none on the palate. The small protractile mouth opens downward into a tube. There may be one or two species of *Drepane*, or perhaps only two color forms. In one form the silver fish has dark markings in the form of vertical stripes; in the other there are vertical rows of spots. The striped form has been called *D. longimana* and the spotted one *D. punctata*. If only one species exists it will have to be called *D. punctata*. This is a very pretty foot-long fish, the silvery body usually reflecting shades of purple and often with golden overtones.

The platacids as adults look very much like the other two subfamilies. There is no obvious separation of spinous and rayed parts of the dorsal fin, making batfishes easily distinguishable from the other subfamilies. The small mouth contains a band of small, movable, tricuspid teeth. The 5-9 dorsal spines increase in height posteriorly and are partially hidden by the heavy scale covering of the fins. The changes with growth are familiar to aquarists. The young have very elongate dorsal and anal fin rays making them taller than long. The proportions change until a body shape more like that of the spadefishes has been reached. Adults are often 12 to 20 inches long.

50. *Drepane punctata* (Linnaeus). A prized food fish occurring from the Red Sea and east African coast to northern Australia and Samoa. It reaches north to Taiwan.

51.
Cirrhitus pinnulatus
(Schneider). Wide-
ranging Indo-Pacific
species. Photo by Dr.
Shih-chieh Shen.
Taiwan. (73.2 mm
standard length)

52.
Amblycirrhitus bimacul
(Jenkins). Another wide
ranging species
occurring from eastern
Africa to the Hawaiian
Islands. Photo by Dr.
Shih-chieh Shen.
Taiwan. (69.3 mm
standard length)

53.
Paracirrhites forsteri
(Schneider). Hawkfishe
usually sit on top of
coral heads and
disappear within them a
the first sign of danger.
Photo by Dr. Shih-chief
Shen. Taiwan. (118.4
mm standard length)

Family CIRRHITIDAE
HAWKFISHES

Hawkfishes are generally small to moderate sized fishes of less than a foot in length. They are elongate-oval, perch-like fishes with a single dorsal fin which is notched between the spiny and soft parts. The pectoral fins have about 14 rays but the lower 5-8 rays are simple and un-branched, usually enlarged, and with the membranes deeply incised so that they are almost separate from the fin. They are usually elongated beyond the rest of the fin. The dorsal fin spines may have one or more cirri projecting from their mem-branes near their tips as can be seen in some of the photos of the species. The mouth is moderate in size, protractile, and provided with bands of sharp teeth. The vomer has teeth, but the palatines may lack them. A fringe is present at the back of the anterior nostril.

Hawkfishes are basically shallow water fishes inhabiting rocky or coral areas that may be in water only a few feet deep. They were easily collected in Hawaii by skin-diving with hand nets. Certain species of the genera *Oxycirrhites* and *Cyprinocirr-hites* have been found in water from 100 feet to over 300 feet deep.

Hawkfishes are commonly imported for the aquarium trade and are known as hardy fishes. They will take a variety of foods although their natural prey is crusta-ceans and small fishes. The common aqua-rium species usually grow to a size of about four to six inches.

The hawkfishes are not considered good food fishes.

54. *Cirrhitichthys falco* Randall. Closely related to *C. serratus* Randall, but differing in details of color pattern. Ranges apparently from Great Barrier Reef of Australia to Taiwan (Randall records it only from the Philip-pines). Photo by Dr. Shih-chieh Shen. Shui-Tai, southern tip of Taiwan. (70.7 mm standard length)

55.
Cirrhitus pinnulatus
(Schneider). Reported
be a nocturnal specie
hiding by day and
coming out to feed a
night. Photo by Dr.
Shih-chieh Shen.
Taiwan. (89.8 mm
standard length)

56.
Cirrhitus pinnulatus
(Schneider). A shallo
water species usually
found in areas subjec
wave action. Photo b
Dr. Shih-chieh Shen.
Taiwan. (82.4 mm
standard length)

57.
Cirrhitus pinnulatus
(Schneider). The col
and pattern are some
what variable, as see
this and the above
photos. Note the lac
spots on the caudal
proper in this smalle
individual. Photo by
Shih-chieh Shen.
Taiwan. (59.8 mm
standard length)

58. *Siganus spinus* (Linnaeus). This species is also known under the name *S. striolata*. It attains a length of 14 inches. Photo by Dr. Shih-chieh Shen. Taiwan. (77 mm standard length)

59. *Siganus oramin* (Bloch and Schneider). A coastal water species which normally has white spots covering the body and a dark shoulder spot. Photo by Dr. Shih-chieh Shen. Tung-Liang, Pescadore Islands. (122.6 mm standard length)

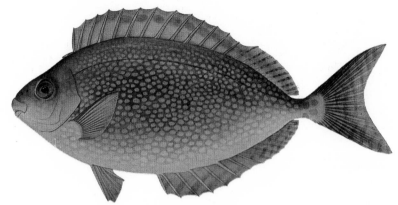

60. *Siganus rostratus* (Valenciennes). Wide-ranging through the Indo-Pacific. Attains a length of over one foot. Illustration by Tomita.

61. *Siganus puellus* (Schlegel). The blue-lined spinefoot or blue-lined rabbitfish occurs from the East Indies to the Gilbert and Solomon Islands and north to the Philippines (and Taiwan?). Illustration by Arita.

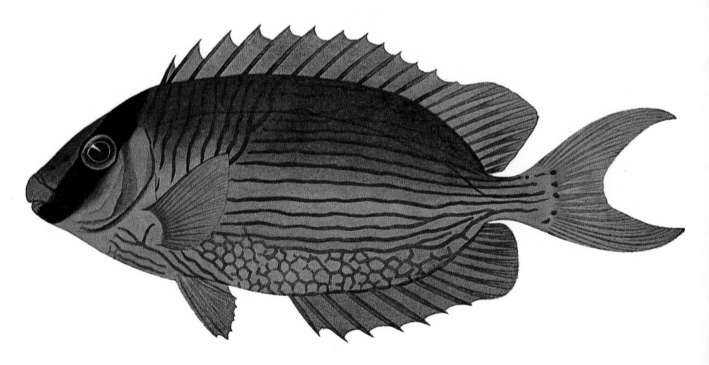

62 & 63.   *Ctenochaetus strigosus* (Bennett). Several species of surgeonfishes have yellow juvenile stages. Besides *C. strigosus* shown here, *Acanthurus coeruleus* (Caribbean), *A. olivaceous*, and *A. pyroferus* are species which show this color as young but have various markings which enable them to be recognized. Photos by Dr. Shih-chieh Shen. Huing-Kuing, southern tip of Taiwan. (68.8 mm standard length)

64. *Paracanthurus hepatus* (Linnaeus). The blue tang usually occurs in small schools around coral. When first introduced into an aquarium they will hide among the rocks or corals provided. Photo by K.H. Choo. Taiwan.

65. *Acanthurus lineatus* (Linnaeus). The blue-lined surgeonfish attains a length of about one foot. Photo by K. H. Choo. Taiwan.

66. *Acanthurus lineatus* (Linnaeus). This species occurs in coastal waters around reefs. Photo by Dr. Shih-chieh Shen. Su-Ho, northeastern part of Taiwan. (57 mm standard length)

67. *Acanthurus lineatus* (Linnaeus). Note that there is some variation in pattern, such as broken or forked lines, in these three photos of the blue-lined surgeonfish. Photo by K.H. Choo. Taiwan.

68. *Zebrasoma scopas* (Cuvier). The juvenile *Z. scopas* rarely is seen in aquarium stores and is often confused with *Z. flavescens* (below). Photo by K.H. Choo. Taiwan.

69. *Zebrasoma flavescens* (Bennett). The white caudal spine stands out against the pure yellow of this fish. Note the lack of white spots. Photo by K.H. Choo. Taiwan.

70. *Zebrasoma scopas* (Cuvier). Although faded, the white spots and lines characteristic of juvenile *Z. scopas* are present. Photo by Dr. Shih-chieh Shen. Taiwan. (37 mm standard length)

71. ?*Zebrasoma flavescens* (Bennett). Although practically identical with the above fish, the lack of spots would cause it to be identified as *Z. flavescens*. Photo by Dr. Shih-chieh Shen. Ho-Pi-Hou, southern tip of Taiwan. (44.9 mm standard length)

72. *Naso unicornis* (Forskal). The unicornfish attains a length of almost two feet. Photo by Dr. Shih-chieh Shen. Taiwan. (107.4 mm standard length)

73. *Zebrasoma scopas* (Cuvier). As this fish grows, the white spots in the posterior part of the body coalesce into horizontal lines. Photo by Dr. Shih-chieh Shen. Wan-li-Tung, southern tip of Taiwan. (127.0 mm standard length)

74. *Naso brevirostris* (Cuvier & Valenciennes). Young *Naso* often look very much alike. Note here the difference in the color pattern between this species' anal fin and the one below. Photo by Dr. Shih-chieh Shen. Wan-li-Tung, southern tip of Taiwan. (97.4 mm standard length)

75. *Naso unicornis* (Forskal). At this size there is no hint that a projecting horn will develop. The adult is shown in Pacific Marine Fishes Book 1, p. 89 (#144). Photo by Dr. Shih-chieh Shen. Nan-Wan, Taiwan. (80 mm standard length)

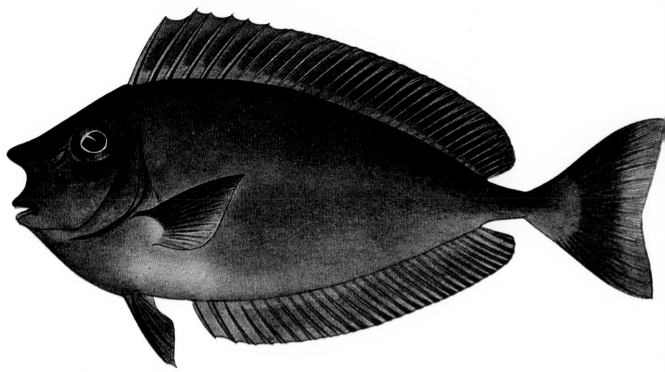

76. *Naso brevirostris* (Cuvier and Valenciennes). The snout horn will grow much larger than this. Illustration by Arita. (about 150 mm standard length)

77. *Naso unicornis* (Forskal). An extremely wide-ranging species occurring from the Red Sea to the Hawaiian Islands. Photo by Dr. Shih-chieh Shen. Pai-Sha, southern tip of Taiwan. (126.6 mm standard length)

78. *Ctenochaetus cyanoguttatus* Randall. A recently described species that has a range from Zanzibar to Cocos Island, Costa Rica. Illustration by Arita.

79. *Naso lituratus* (Bloch and Schneider). This species attains a length of about 20 inches. Photo by K.H. Choo. Taiwan.

80. *Zanclus canescens* (Linnaeus). Moorish idols are fairly easily collected at night with a hand net. During the day, however, it is difficult to approach them. Photo by K.H. Choo. Taiwan.

81. *Zanclus canescens* (Linnaeus). The dorsal filament is often damaged in shipping but will grow back in time. Photo by K.H. Choo. Taiwan.

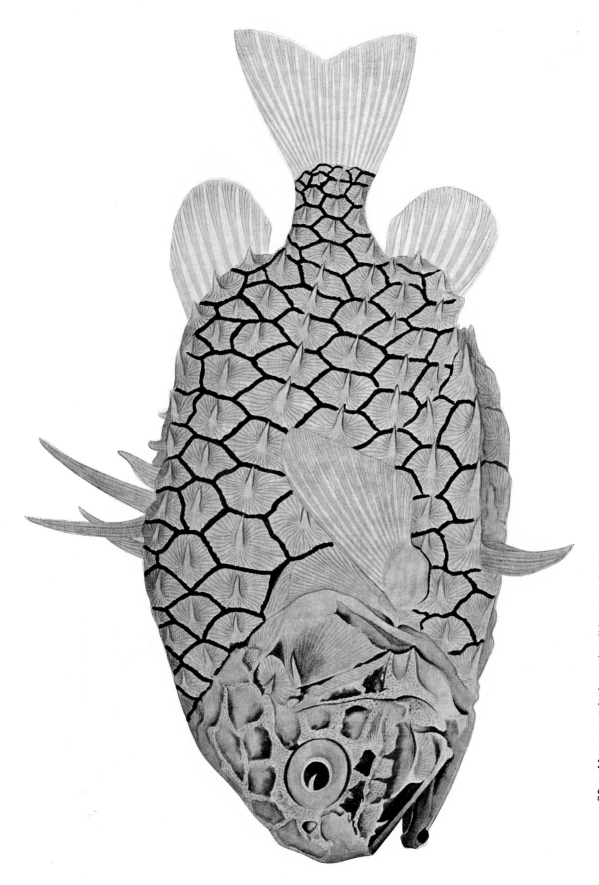

82. *Monocentris japonica* (Houttuyn). The black spot near the symphysis of the lower jaw contains symbiotic phosphorescent bacteria. This phosphorescence is well known in the pinecone fish. Illustration by Arita.

83. *Monocentris japonica* (Houttuyn). Fairly common in Japan. Occurs in schools around rocky areas. Photo by K.H. Choo. Taiwan.

84. *Monocentris japonica* (Houttuyn). Attains a length of about 160 mm and is eaten fried, toasted or in soup. Photo by K.H. Choo. Taiwan.

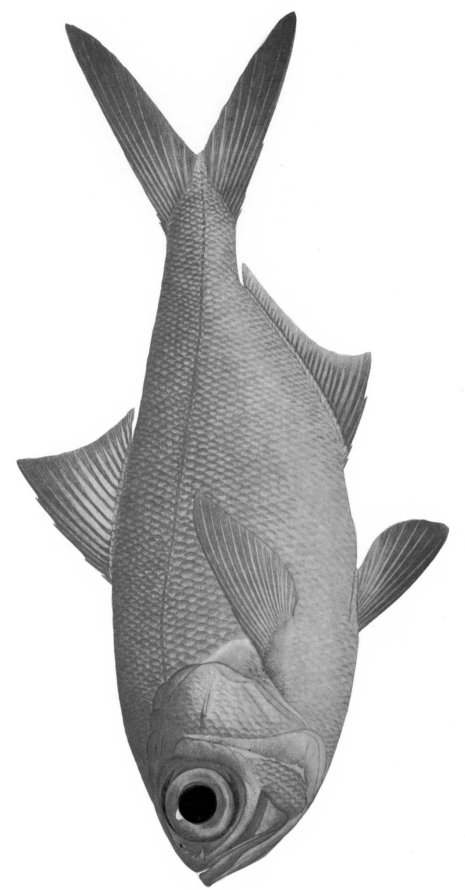

85. *Beryx splendens* Lowe. This species is caught in depths of some 300-400 meters in Japan. Known from Japan to Australia and New Zealand and has been recorded from the Atlantic. Illustration by Kumada.

Family BERYCIDAE
ALFONCINOS

Alfoncinos are primitive berycomorph deep water oceanic fishes related to the holocentrids. They differ from the squirrelfishes in having a shorter, deeper body and fewer dorsal fin spines.

The compressed body is oblong to ovate, covered with either normal cycloid or ctenoid scales or scales which may be granular or foliate. The eyes are large, as is the mouth. The oblique mouth is provided with villiform bands of teeth; the palatines and vomer are also with teeth. The single dorsal fin is composed of 2-8 weak spines and about a dozen soft rays, and the anal fin has 2-4 spines. The pelvic fins contain one spine and seven rays. The caudal fin is forked.

Beryx splendens is a two-foot long bright red fish that occurs in waters below 1,000 feet and possibly as deep as 2,000 or more feet. It is considered a food fish in Japan, where it is taken among rocks at depths of 300 to 400 meters. The related species *B. decadactylus* is deeper bodied and has fewer lateral line scales but more dorsal fin rays. It is also caught in deep water with *B. splendens*. Both these species have been reported from the northern Atlantic as well as the Japanese area. For the first year or more young *Beryx* are midwater fishes, adopting the bottom-dwelling habitat of the adults late in life.

The nannygai of Australia, *Trachichthodes affinis*, grows to about 18 inches. The name nannygai is an aboriginal name also applied to *Glaucosoma scapulare*.

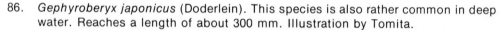
86.   *Gephyroberyx japonicus* (Doderlein). This species is also rather common in deep water. Reaches a length of about 300 mm. Illustration by Tomita.

87. *Kyphosus lembus* (Cuvier). The large-tailed drummer may be found feeding on algae around coral reefs. Illustration by Arita. (to 14 inches)

88. *Kyphosus cinerascens* (Forskal). Feeds on the algae of reefs. Normally found in shallower coastal waters. Illustration by Tomita. (to 18 inches)

Family KYPHOSIDAE
RUDDERFISHES AND NIBBLERS

The rudderfishes have compressed oval bodies, but are still heavily built. The mouth is small, terminal, and slightly to moderately protractile. The single dorsal fin is usually continuous or at most slightly divided. It contains about 10 or 11 spines and 10-15 rays. The anal fin is similarly shaped but shorter, with 3 spines and about 11-13 rays. The scales are moderate on the sides and become smaller around the periphery of the fish. The vertical fins are also covered with small scales. The dorsal fin folds back into this scaly sheath.

As mentioned in Book 5 (p. 433), the adults are inhabitants of rocky or reef areas. The young, however, are often found in the more open waters around floating sargassum weed. They are able to change their color to a mottled pattern which closely resembles the sargassum, providing additional protection from predators. These small chubs or rudderfishes make good aquarium fishes. They will remain near the surface of the water, swimming back and forth unless provided with some substitute for the sargassum. Feed them with plant material, perhaps with some crustaceans mixed in from time to time.

Rudderfishes are said to be good game fishes. Their flesh is palatable and, at least for some species, quite good. One Pacific species has been reported to cause "colorful dreams" when eaten. Whether this is an attribute of the fish itself or possibly some reaction due to spoilage is not known.

Most of the species of the genus *Kyphosus* are morphologically similar, making them difficult to distinguish. The species with which we are concerned are silvery gray with lighter lines along the scale rows. The species are distinguished by such things as scale counts, fin proportions, silvery markings below each eye, etc.

89. *Kyphosus cinerascens* (Forskal). The silvery band below the eye is one of the characteristics of this species. Photo by Dr. Shih-chieh Shen. Taiwan. (92 mm standard length)

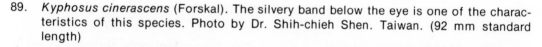

90.
Leiognathus equulus
(Forskal). An abundant
fish in bays and will
enter the brackish
waters of estuaries.
Photo by Dr. Shih-chieh
Shen. Taiwan. (102.2
mm standard length)

91.
Leiognathus rivulatus
(Temminck and
Schlegel). This species
occurs in more offshore
and deeper waters than
the preceding. Photo by
Dr. Shih-chieh Shen.
Taiwan. (120.0 mm
standard length)

92.
Leiognathus rivulatus
(Temminck and
Schlegel). Ranges from
southern Japan to Korea
and Taiwan. In Japan
spawning occurs in
May. Photo by Dr. Shih-
chieh Shen. Taiwan.
(88.2 mm standard
length)

Family LEIOGNATHIDAE
PONYFISH OR SLIPMOUTHS

Slipmouths are small fishes usually less than six inches in length (but sometimes reaching 10 inches) inhabiting tropical and subtropical areas of the Indo-Pacific region. They are basically marine fishes but sometimes may be encountered in brackish or even fresh water. Large schools are seen in shallow water near beaches or estuaries.

The deep, elongate-oval body is strongly compressed. The dorsal and anal fins are similarly shaped and both fold back into scaly basal sheaths. The caudal fin is forked and the small pelvic fins are thoracic in position and provided with a large scaly axillary process. The mouth is small and highly protractile, forming a tube. The common name slipmouth arose from the protrusible mouth, and the name ponyfish supposedly refers to the appearance of the head with the mouth extended. The tube formed by the mouth may point upward or downward. The teeth may be setiform and arranged in bands or larger and more canine-like. The palate is toothless. Slipmouths are usually silvery in color with some dark irregular markings dorsally.

In South Africa these fishes are called slimys or soapys due to the slimy mucus excreted from glands on the body. Upon handling, this mucus is excreted in large quantities. They are not necessarily good food fish but are easily caught in large numbers, are easily dried in the sun, and are edible.

It has been reported that there is luminous tissue present around the area where the esophagus meets the stomach. The very compressed body permits the viewing of this luminescence when the fishes are handled.

The principal genera are *Leiognathus*, *Secutor*, *Gazza*, and *Equula*. These are distinguished by type of teeth, direction of the mouth-tube when open, and extent of lateral line and scale covering.

93.   *Secutor ruconius* (Hamilton-Buchanan). The pug-nosed ponyfish is found more commonly in river mouths. It attains a length of a little over three inches. Photo by Dr. Shih-chieh Shen. Taiwan. (47 mm standard length)

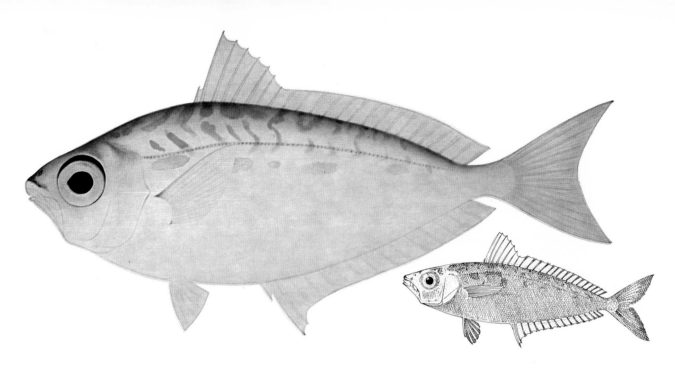

94. *Leiognathus rivulatus* (Temminck and Schlegel), and *L. elongatus* Smith and Pope (insert). Both are slender bodied but can be distinguished by head shape. Illustration by Tomita.

95. *Leiognathus equulus* (Forskal) and *L. dussumieri* Cuvier and Valenciennes (insert). Both species are considered good eating even though little flesh can be obtained from the compressed bodies. Illustration by Kumada.

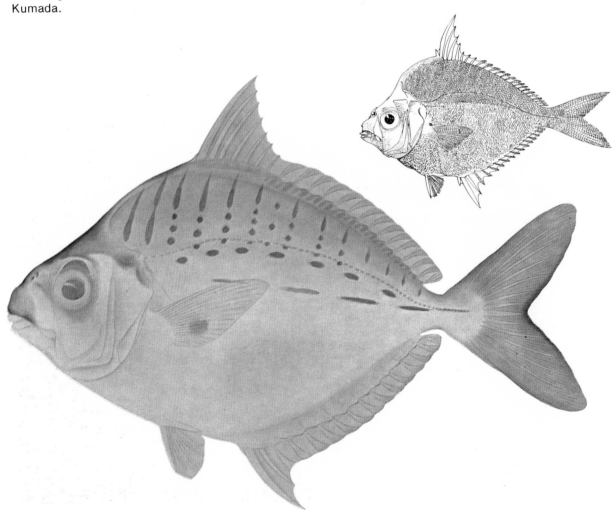

Family MENIDAE
MOONFISH

The family Menidae is composed of a single genus and species of fish, *Mene maculata*. It is easily recognizable and identified by its flat, nearly triangular body, with a sharp abdomen. The mouth is small but protractile, forming an upwardly directed tube when open. The teeth in the jaws are villiform; no teeth are present on the bones of the palate. The dorsal fin is without spines in the adult but contains nine spines in the young. The anal fin is normal in the young, having two spines and numerous rays. With age the spines disappear and the rays become reduced and embedded in the skin. The pelvic fins have the normal complement of one spine and five rays and is filamentous in the juveniles, the first ray remaining long and flattened in the adult. The pectoral fins are normally shaped and the caudal fin is forked. The body is covered with many minute scales.

The moonfish or razor-trevally is widely distributed in the Indo-Pacific region. It inhabits the deeper coastal waters, but occasionally juveniles may be found closer to shore and even in estuaries.

These small (to about eight inches in length) fishes are usually placed in taxonomic proximity to the slipmouths or Leiognathidae and have been reported to be somewhat intermediate between these and the jacks or carangids. The common name razor-trevally refers to the resemblance of this fish to the trevallies or jacks of the family Carangidae. The razor part of the name of course refers to the extremely sharp abdominal edge. The thickness of this fish is such that if it is placed in the air it will quickly dry out.

Although a very interesting species, the moonfish will probably not be available for the marine aquarist. It is probably a carnivore, eating small fishes and invertebrates of the open waters.

96. *Mene maculata* (Bloch and Schneider). Occurs in the warm oceanic waters of the Indo-Pacific. Photo by Dr. Shih-chieh Shen. Taiwan. (125.2 mm standard length)

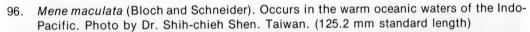

97. *Mene maculata* (Bloch and Schneider). The dorsal and anal spines are only visible in the young stages of the spotted moonfish. Illustration by Tomita. (to 200 mm)

Family FORMIONIDAE
FORMIONIDS

The formionids are poorly known fishes that have been shifted around from family to family but are now considered a full family. The genus *Formio* was once known as *Apolectus* but had to be changed due to this latter name being preoccupied. It was once placed in with the genus *Stromateus*, which it superficially resembles, and again by others in with the Carangidae.

Apparently a single genus and species, *Formio niger*, is known. It is distributed throughout the Indo-Pacific but little has been written about it. The body is deep and the scales small. A few scales are modified into scutes at the end of the lateral line. The dorsal and anal fins are shaped somewhat like those of the bramids, and the spines of these fins are few and rudimentary. The pelvic fins are absent.

Formio are occasionally found in shallow waters where they are netted. They are an excellent food fish. According to J.L.B. Smith, they swim on their side a few feet below the surface, looking like large "silvery discs." Occurs in schools.

98. *Formio niger* (Bloch). A rare and rather deep water fish around Japan, but reported as a shallow water fish occurring in large shoals along parts of the African coast. Photo by Dr. Shih-chieh Shen. Tam-Shui, northern tip of Taiwan. (230.6 mm standard length)

Family BRAMIDAE
POMFRETS, FANFISHES

The pomfrets are relatively large fishes of the open oceans. They are widely distributed in temperate and tropical waters, often at considerable depths. The zones that they inhabit are called the mesopelagic, which is approximately 200 to 1,000 meters from the surface, and the bathypelagic, which extends from 1,000 to 4,000 meters in depth. It is easy to see that these fishes, although locally abundant at times, are not often seen except by scientists and perhaps fishermen who trawl at these depths.

Their body is usually deep, oval-shaped, and strongly compressed. The head is blunt, and the body tapers to a slender caudal peduncle. The single dorsal and anal fins are similarly shaped, with the anterior part higher than the rest. There may be two to three unbranched rays preceding each of these fins. The pectoral fins are long and pointed (falcate) and the caudal fin deeply forked (lunate). An axillary scaly process accompanies the pelvic fins. The scales are of moderate size (with some variations) and may have ridges which together form longitudinal lines on the sides of the fish. The mouth is moderate, oblique, and provided with bands of fine, slender teeth in the jaws.

Considerable changes occur with age in this group of fishes, and there are many problems still to be worked out. The young may have more elongate fins and a completely different body shape. In addition, they have spiny heads. The scale ridges of

99. *Brama* sp. (possibly *B. raii* or *B. japonica*). Oceanic fishes of moderate depths. Some attain sizes of more than two feet. Photo by Dr. Shih-chieh Shen. Taiwan. (150.9 mm standard length)

100. *Centropholis petersi* Hilgendorf. A beautiful fish that unfortunately is uncommon. It inhabits moderately deep oceanic waters. Illustration by Arita.

the adults are spines in the juveniles, and the teeth of the vomer and palatine bones are lost with age.

In coloration these fishes are usually either blackish or silvery.

Due to their pelagic habitat and the taxonomic problems that are still unsettled, the pomfrets and breams are poorly known. Even the famous Ray's bream (*Brama raii* or *Brama brama*) is not that well known. The Pacific form has been called *Brama japonica*. This latter fish, if it is truly a distinct species, is reported as widespread in the northern Pacific from southern California to Alaska and along the western Pacific coast of Asia to Japan and vicinity. It has also been reported from the tropical mid-Pacific. It is a good food fish but the problem would be to catch it in enough quantity to make it commercially profitable. They appear to be caught nearer the surface in the mid-north Pacific in early summer and further north by late summer. This may not be a migration but a temperature-related phenomenon wherein the fishes move closer to or away from the surface as it cools off or warms up. In other areas this fish appears sporadically, possibly depending upon the vagaries of water temperature.

As far as known, the food of *Brama japonica* consists of fish, squid, and crustaceans. It attains a length of approximately one meter.

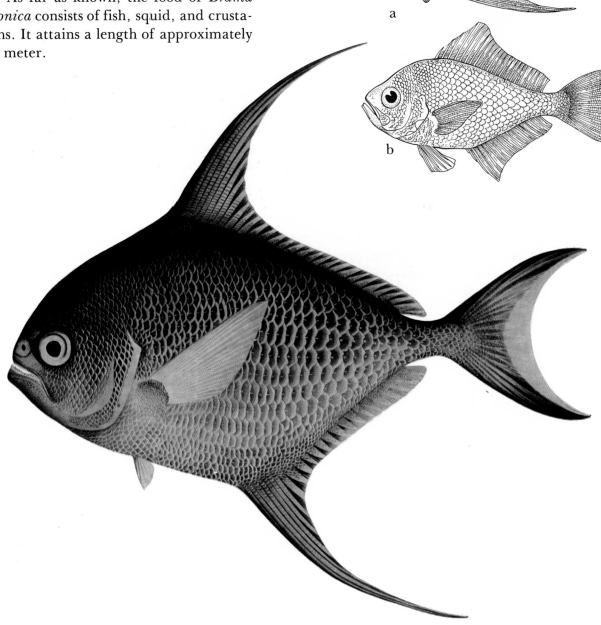

101.　*Taractes longipinnis* (Lowe). As compared with two closely related species, (a) *T. steindachneri* (Doderlein) and (b) *T. platycephalus* Matsubara. Attains a length of about three feet. Illustration by Kumada.

The Atlantic species, *Brama brama* or Ray's bream, is smaller, reaching a length of only about 40-50 cm, or half that of *Brama japonica*. It is a mesopelagic species inhabiting the northeastern Atlantic. Its appearance is also sporadic and, although the flesh is good, it connot support a large commercial fishery. The same phenomenon of their position being directed by the prevailing temperatures seems to occur. Commercial quantities are taken by trawls and long-lines off the Spanish coast about the middle of winter.

Little is known about the biology of this species other than spawning occurs at temperatures above 20° C. Young fishes may be taken by net in the mid-Atlantic. The food of Ray's bream consists of squids, fish, and crustaceans, much the same as that of *Brama japonica*.

Another genus normally attributed to this family is *Taractes*.

The pteraclids or fanfishes share many characteristics with the bramids but are considered by some a separate family, the Pteraclidae. Members of this group have a compressed body tapering to a small caudal peduncle. They have scales with ridges which form lines along the side of the fish and each scale is attached to the one before it by a modified spine. The mouth is moderate, oblique and the jaws provided with small teeth. Two unusual anatomical features of these fishes are the position of the vent (at the throat) and the size of the dorsal and anal fins. As the common name suggests, the fins are fan-like. They are very large, almost equal in shape, and provided with 40-50 rays each. The genera are separated by the position of the origin of the dorsal fin, whether it starts on the snout or behind it.

Like the bramids, the fanfishes are inhabitants of the open oceans, are perhaps to be considered fairly rare, and are almost never brought up alive. A fanfish in an aquarium would be a spectacular display, the sooty black fins contrasting sharply with the shining silvery body.

Family POLYMIXIIDAE
BEARDFISHES

This small deep water family is placed in the order Beryciformes, which contains better known fishes such as the berycids, monocentrids, and holocentrids (squirrelfishes). The beardfishes are distinctive enough, however, to merit their own suborder, the Polymixioidei. There is a single genus, *Polymixia*, and only two or three species.

The body is somewhat elongate and slightly compressed. The head is moderate and the mouth large. Both palate and jaw contain villiform teeth. The single dorsal fin is higher in front and contains about 5 spines and 25-40 rays. The anal fin is similarly shaped but with a much shorter base. The ventral fins have one spine and 6 or 7 rays. Percoid fishes most usually have one spine and 5 rays. Perhaps the most obvious distinguishing feature of the beardfishes, and the basis for the common name, is the barbels located on the chin. The Spanish name barbudo has been attached to these fishes—barbudo in Spanish means bearded. Another characteristic which helps distinguish this group from the holocentrids is the smaller, more numerous scales. It is also interesting to note that the name *Polymixia* is roughly translated as many (*poly*) mixing (*myxia*), referring to a mixing of the characters of many forms.

The species of the family include *Polymixia nobilis*, *P. lowei*, and *P. japonica*, although this is subject to change when these fishes are studied more thoroughly. *Polymixia nobilis* may be found at depths of approximately 200-400 meters around the African coast. Off Japan this species is reported as abundant in deep water. It is not considered a good food fish but is used for fish-cakes in Japan. It attains a length of about 500 mm and may spawn in the early spring. This species is widespread in the Indo-Pacific and has been reported from the Atlantic, but the Atlantic species appears to be *P. lowei*.

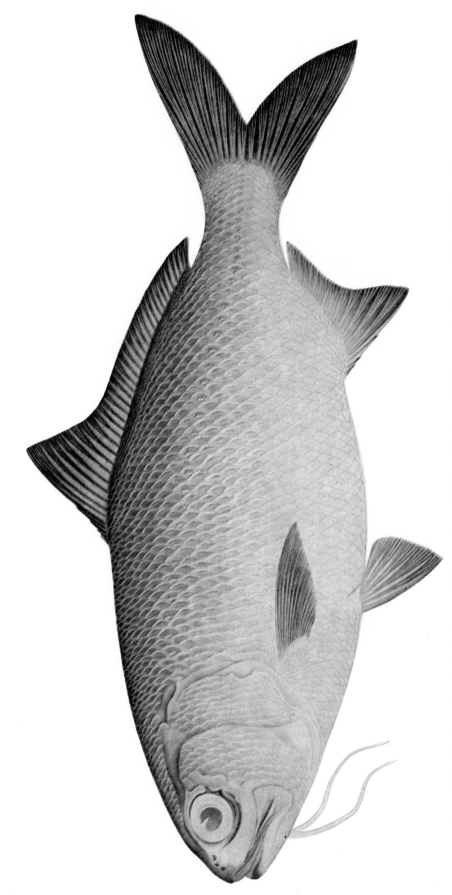

102. *Polymixia japonica* Steindachner. Although *Polymixia* has barbels which resemble those of the Mullidae, they are structurally different. Illustration by Arita.

103. *Eleutheronema tetradactylum* (Shaw). A shallow water fish that reaches a length of about 4 feet. Illustration by Arita.

104. *Scatophagus argus* (Boddaert). Adults. The number of species in this genus is still undecided. Photo by Dr. Herbert R. Axelrod.

105. *Scatophagus argus* (Boddaert). The reddish coloration has prompted this variety to be called *S. rubrifrons*. It may be a juvenile character. Photo by Dr. Shih-chieh Shen. Kee-Lung, northern tip of Taiwan. (23.6 mm standard length)

106. *Scatophagus argus* (Boddaert). Common in estuaries, even entering rivers. Attains a length of about one foot. Photo by Dr. Shih-chieh Shen. Taiwan. (97.2 mm standard length)

107. *Scatophagus argus* (Boddaert). This is one fish both marine and freshwater aquarists can enjoy, as it can be acclimated to either medium. Photo by Dr. Shih-chieh Shen. Kee-Lung, northern tip of Taiwan. (48.5 mm standard length)

108. *Microcanthus strigatus* (Cuvier and Valenciennes). The stripey is found from Hawaii to China and Japan, the Philippines, and Australia. Photo by Dr. Shih-chieh Shen. (100 mm standard length)

109. *Microcanthus strigatus* (Cuvier and Valenciennes). A hardy fish suitable for the beginning marine aquarist. Photo by K.H. Choo. Taiwan.

110. *Chaetodon ephippium* Cuvier. The saddled butterflyfish is one of the more colorful of these fishes. It reaches a length of about one foot. Photo by K.H. Choo. Taiwan.

111. *Chaetodon ephippium* Cuvier. Butterflyfishes on occasion have the first few dorsal fin spines missing or deformed, as this one shows. Photo by Dr. Shih-chieh Shen. Kee-Lung, northern tip of Taiwan. (124.5 mm standard length)

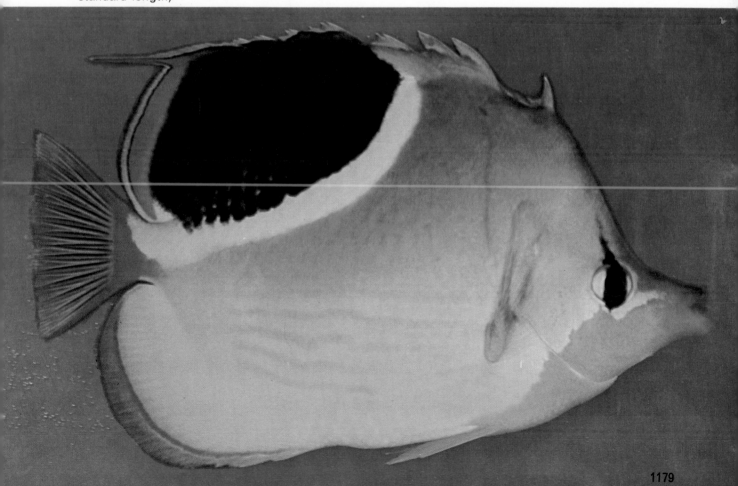

112. *Chaetodon plebeius* Cuvier. The two-spot butterflyfish is an ideal size for the marine aquarium. It will grow to slightly over four inches. Photo by K.H. Choo. Taiwan.

113. *Chaetodon plebeius* Cuvier. The spot on the side is highly variable in shape and color. The blue quickly fades, in some cases leaving a brownish spot or no spot at all. Photo by Dr. Shih-chieh Shen. Banana Bay, southern tip of Taiwan. (52.4 mm standard length)

114. *Chaetodon ornatissimus* Cuvier. One of the prettiest of butterflyfishes, the ornate butterflyfish is also very difficult to keep. Photo by K.H. Choo. Taiwan.

115. *Chaetodon plebeius* Cuvier. The pigment of the eye band in the eye itself is reflecting light, here making the eye more discernable than usual. Photo by Dr. Shih-chieh Shen. Nan-Wan, southern tip of Taiwan. (41.3 mm standard length)

116. *Chaetodon melannotus* Bloch and Schneider. The name "*melannotus*" means black back. This characteristic is clearly shown in this photo. Photo by Dr. Shih-chieh Shen. Taiwan. (92.4 mm standard length)

117. *Chaetodon melannotus* Bloch and Schneider. The juveniles are similar to the adults except for slight changes in the color pattern. Photo by K.H. Choo. Taiwan.

118. *Chaetodon semeion* Bleeker. One of the larger butterflyfishes, reaching a length of about 10 inches or more. Photo by K.H. Choo. Taiwan.

119. *Chaetodon semeion* Bleeker. Adults possess a long filament extending from the dorsal fin. Photo by Dr. Shih-chieh Shen. Banana Bay, southern tip of Taiwan. (145.8 mm standard length)

120. *Chaetodon xanthurus* Bleeker. Shipments from the Philippine Islands will often contain a few of these butterflyfishes. Photo by Dr. Shih-chieh Shen. Taiwan. (94 mm standard length)

121. *Chaetodon xanthurus* Bleeker. Another small sized butterflyfish, not reaching a size larger than about 5 inches. Photo by K.H. Choo. Taiwan.

122. *Chaetodon wiebeli* Kaup. A Southeast Asian butterflyfish that is not too often seen in aquarium shops. Photo by K.H. Choo. Taiwan.

123. *Chaetodon wiebeli* Kaup. The mask of this species is distinctive and makes it easily recognizable. Photo by Dr. Shih-chieh Shen. Haing-Tsai-Kung, southern tip of Taiwan. (136.4 mm standard length)

124.	*Chaetodon octofasciatus* Bloch. The name "*octofasciatus*" means eight stripes, referring to the pattern of this species (the last stripe is on the edge of the dorsal and anal fins). Photo by Dr. Shih-chieh Shen. Tung-Liang, Pescadore Islands. (81 mm standard length)

125.	*Chaetodon octofasciatus* Bloch. Although the range centers around Southeast Asia, this species extends into the Indian Ocean to the waters around India. Photo by K.H. Choo. Taiwan.

126. *Chaetodon bennetti* Cuvier. This colorful butterflyfish is uncommon, and its appearances in aquarium stores are few and far between. Photo by Dr. Shih-chieh Shen. Ao-Luan-Bi, southern tip of Taiwan. (152.4 mm standard length)

127. *Chaetodon octofasciatus* Bloch. This species is relatively small, the maximum length being about 4 inches. Photo by K.H. Choo. Taiwan.

128. *Chaetodon lunula* (Lacepede). Adult. A fairly common and hardy species that would be recommended as a beginning butterflyfish. Photo by Dr. Shih-chieh Shen. Taiwan. (138 mm standard length)

129. *Chaetodon vagabundus* Linnaeus. The vagabond butterflyfish is also common and hardy. It ranges throughout the tropical Indo-Pacific. Photo by K.H. Choo. Taiwan.

130. *Chaetodon lunula* (Lacepede). Sub-adult. The head pattern is already formed. The posterior markings are still partly juvenile in character. Photo by Dr. Shih-chieh Shen. Ho-Wan-Li, southern tip of Taiwan. (82 mm standard length)

131. *Chaetodon lunula* (Lacepede). Sub-adult. Slightly younger than the fish in the above photo; this individual shows the head and shoulder pattern less well developed. Photo by K.H. Choo. Taiwan.

132. *Chaetodon unimaculatus* Bloch. The ocellated spot is characteristic of this species. Photo by Dr. Shih-chieh Shen. Taiwan. (63.8 mm standard length)

133. *Chaetodon unimaculatus* Bloch. The one-spot butterflyfish gets fairly large, more than 8 inches, in its natural habitat. Photo by K.H. Choo. Taiwan.

134. *Chaetodon speculum* Cuvier. This species should not be confused with *C. unimaculatus*, which also has a lateral spot. Photo by K.H. Choo. Taiwan.

135. *Chaetodon adiergastos* Seale. Occasionally imported from the Philippine Islands. Note the shape of the eye band. Photo by K.H. Choo. Taiwan.

136. *Chaetodon baronessa* Cuvier. A delicate species occurring in the central and western tropical Pacific. Photo by Dr. Shih-chieh Shen. (40.6 mm standard length)

137. *Chaetodon lineolatus* Cuvier. This is the largest species of butterflyfish (genus *Chaetodon*). It attains a length of over one foot. Photo by Dr. Shih-chieh Shen. Banana Bay, southern tip of Taiwan. (213.3 mm standard length)

138. *Chaetodon lineolatus* Cuvier. On the reef this species is almost always seen in pairs. Photo by Dr. Shih-chieh Shen. Taiwan. (201.2 mm standard length)

139. *Chaetodon lineolatus* Cuvier. Sub-adult. There is very little difference between this stage and the adult (above). Photo by K.H. Choo. Taiwan.

140. *Chaetodon argentatus* Smith and Radcliffe. More typically a Japanese species, but extends as far south as the Philippine Islands. Photo by K.H. Choo. Taiwan.

141. *Chaetodon argentatus* Smith and Radcliffe. Notice the resemblance of this species to *C. xanthurus*. Photo by Dr. Shih-chieh Shen. Wan-li-Tung, southern tip of Taiwan. (87.3 mm standard length)

142. *Chaetodon punctatofasciatus* Cuvier. This species is not often seen in aquarium shops, perhaps because it is more commonly found in water deeper than 30 feet. Photo by K.H. Choo. Taiwan.

143. *Chaetodon punctatofasciatus* Cuvier. The scientific name of this fish is often incorrectly hyphenated as *punctato-fasciatus*. Photo by Dr. Shih-chieh Shen. Huing-Tsai-Kuing, southern tip of Taiwan. (73 mm standard length)

144.
Chaetodon modestus
(Schlegel). Juvenile.
Chaetodon modestus
is common around
southern Japan but
becomes scarcer further
south. Photo by Dr.
Shih-chieh Shen.
Taiwan. (47 mm
standard length)

145. *Chaetodon kleini* Bloch. A widespread and common species but unfortunately not as popular as most butterflyfishes. Photo by K.H. Choo. Taiwan.

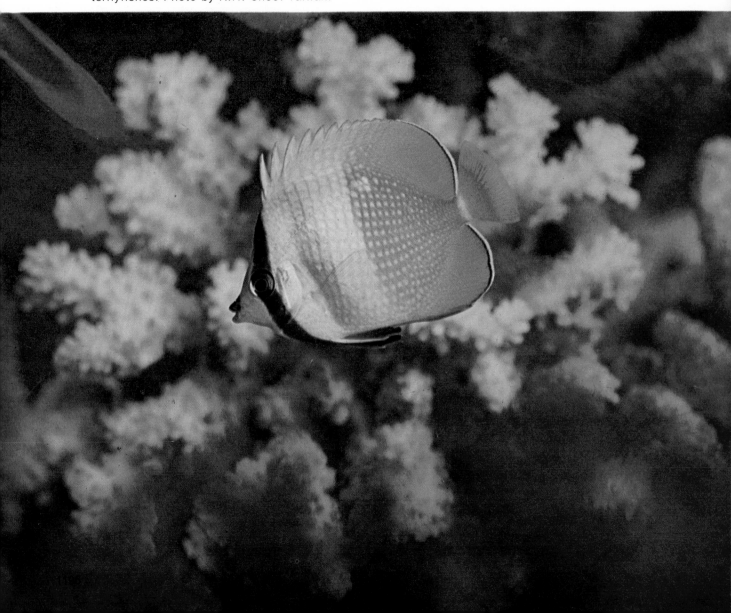

146. *Chaetodon kleini* Bloch. The light band near the center of the body is variable and may even be absent, depending upon the disposition of the individual. Photo by Dr. Shih-chieh Shen. Taiwan. (92 mm standard length)

147. *Chaetodon kleini* Bloch. A slight touch of blue can be seen in the upper part of the eye band. This is normally present but rarely appears in photographs. Photo by K.H. Choo. Taiwan.

148. *Chaetodon citrinellus* Cuvier. The spots on the scales vary in color depending upon the light reflected. Photo by Dr. Shih-chieh Shen. Taiwan. (94.1 mm standard length)

149. *Chaetodon citrinellus* Cuvier. A common but not hardy species. It does not appear too often in dealers' tanks. Photo by K.H. Choo. Taiwan.

150. *Chaetodon guentheri* Ahl. A rare but relatively wide ranging species. Named for Albert Gunther, a prominent scientist of the mid 1800's. Photo by Dr. Shih-chieh Shen. Tsian-Shan, southern tip of Taiwan. (43.2 mm standard length)

151. *Chaetodon citrinellus* Cuvier. This species differs from other spotted butterflyfishes in having a black band along the anal fin. Photo by Dr. Shih-chieh Shen. Taiwan. (84.8 mm standard length)

152. *Chaetodon rafflesi* Bennett. Raffles butterflyfish attains a length of about 5 inches. Photo by K.H. Choo. Taiwan.

153. *Chaetodon reticulatus* Cuvier. Juvenile. The mailed butterflyfish gets quite large, attaining a length of about 8 inches or more. Photo by Dr. Shih-chieh Shen. Kee-Lung, northern tip of Taiwan. (60.4 mm standard length)

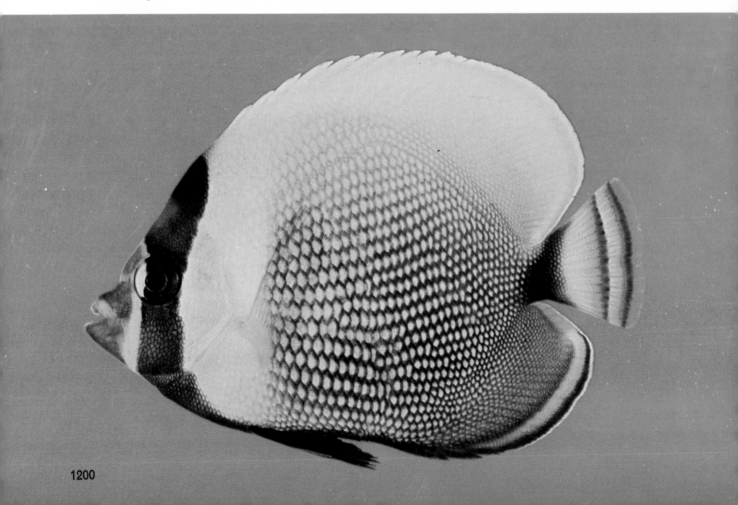

154. *Chaetodon rafflesi* Bennett. Not uncommon around coral reefs and occasionally imported for the marine aquarist. Photo by K.H. Choo. Taiwan.

155. *Chaetodon rafflesi* Bennett. Juvenile. Raffles' butterflyfish is almost always seen in pairs on the reef. Photo by Dr. Shih-chieh Shen. Kee-Lung, northern tip of Taiwan. (45 mm standard length)

156. *Chaetodon trifascialis* Quoy and Gaimard. Adult. Notice the lack of the black bar in the posterior end of the fish. Photo by Dr. Shih-chieh Shen. Taiwan. (92 mm standard length)

157. *Chaetodon trifascialis* Quoy and Gaimard. Juvenile. There is a great difference in the color pattern between juvenile and adult. Photo by Dr. Shih-chieh Shen. Kee-Lung, northern tip of Taiwan. (45 mm standard length)

158. *Chaetodon trifasciatus* Mungo Park. Adult. A common butterflyfish but very delicate. To get one to feed in captivity is a true accomplishment. Photo by Dr. Shih-chieh Shen. Taiwan. (85.6 mm standard length)

159. *Chaetodon trifasciatus* Mungo Park. Juvenile. Perhaps better luck might be encountered if juveniles rather than adults were tried. Juveniles generally adapt to aquarium conditions more rapidly. Photo by Dr. Shih-chieh Shen. Taiwan. (31.7 mm standard length)

160. *Chaetodon ulietensis* Cuvier. The range of this species is the central and western Pacific Ocean. Photo by Dr. Shih-chieh Shen. Taiwan. (122.8 mm standard length)

161. *Chaetodon ulietensis* Cuvier. Adult. The name "*ulietensis*" was derived from the Pacific island where it was discovered, Ulietea. Photo by K.H. Choo. Taiwan.

162. *Chaetodon ulietensis* Cuvier. Juvenile. There is not much difference between the juvenile and adult of this species. Photo by Dr. Shih-chieh Shen. Kee-Lung, northern tip of Taiwan. (26.6 mm standard length)

163. *Chaetodon auriga* Forskal. Sub-adult. The characteristic dorsal fin filament will soon make its appearance in this individual. Photo by K.H. Choo. Taiwan.

164. *Heniochus varius*
(Cuvier). Adult. Both
nape and supraorbital
protrusions are
developed. Photo by Dr.
Shih-chieh Shen.
Taiwan. (131.5 mm
standard length)

165. *Heniochus varius* (Cuvier). Juvenile. Neither supraorbital horns nor nape bump are developed at this stage.
Photo by Dr. Shih-chieh Shen. Kee-Lung, northern tip of Taiwan. (38.5 mm standard length)

166. *Heniochus varius* (Cuvier). Species of this genus make good aquarium inhabitants. Photo by K.H. Choo. Taiwan.

167. *Heniochus varius* (Cuvier). A medium-sized butterflyfish reaching a length of about 9 inches.
Photo by K.H. Choo. Taiwan.

168. *Heniochus acuminatus* (Linnaeus). The coachman, as this fish is commonly called, is probably the most common species of this genus in the aquarium trade. Photo by K.H. Choo. Taiwan.

169.
Heniochus acuminatus
(Linnaeus). Juvenile.
This individual is
probably recently trans-
formed from the pelagic
larval stage. Photo by
Dr. Shih-chieh Shen.
Kee-Lung, northern tip
of Taiwan. (25 mm
standard length)

170.   *Heniochus monoceros*
Cuvier. Juvenile. The masked
butterflyfish is less common
than the other species, but will
occasionally be offered for sale.
Photo by Dr. Shih-chieh Shen.
Taiwan. (46.5 mm standard
length)

171.
Heniochus singularius
Smith and Radcliffe.
Adult. This species
grows quite large for a
butterflyfish, reaching a
length of about one foot.
Photo by Dr. Shih-chieh
Shen. Taiwan. (92.8 mm
standard length)

172. *Heniochus singularius* Smith and Radcliffe. Sub-adult. Probably the rarest of the species of *Heniochus*. Its care is similar to that of the other species. Photo by Dr. Shih-chieh Shen. Kee-Lung, northern tip of Taiwan. (68 mm standard length)

173. *Heniochus chrysostomus* Cuvier. Sub-adult. This species is commonly found as pairs on the reef. Photo by Dr. Shih-chieh Shen. Kee-Lung, northern tip of Taiwan. (79 mm standard length)

174. *Heniochus chrysostomus* Cuvier. A fairly hardy species that is often available to marine aquarists. Photo by Dr. Shih-chieh Shen. Kee-Lung, northern tip of Taiwan. (79 mm standard length)

175. *Hemitaurichthys polylepis* (Bleeker). Large schools of *Hemitaurichthys polylepis* are seen hovering over the reefs in Hawaii and Eniwetok. Photo by Dr. Shih-chieh Shen. Taiwan. (77.8 mm standard length)

176. *Hemitaurichthys polylepis* (Bleeker). This species does not take well to captivity. Mostly large individuals are offered for sale. Photo by K.H. Choo. Taiwan.

177. *Forcipiger flavissimus* Jordan and McGregor. Long-nosed butterflyfishes do well in aquaria. Their antics are a source of pleasure for marine aquarists. Photo by Dr. Shih-chieh Shen. Taiwan. (138 mm standard length)

178. *Forcipiger flavissimus* Jordan and McGregor. Long-nosed butterflyfishes grow to a size of more than 7 inches. Photo by K.H. Choo. Taiwan.

179. *Histiopterus acutirostris* (Temminck and Schlegel). This species ranges from southern Japan to Korea. The closely related species *Histiopterus typus* Temminck and Schlegel (insert) is more widely distributed. These species are also known under the generic name *Evistias*. Illustration by Arita.

Family PENTACEROTIDAE
ARMORHEADS OR BOARFISHES

The boarfishes or armorheads are moderate sized fishes inhabiting the cool deeper waters of all oceans. Most species are found in the Indo-Pacific region.

These fishes have compressed bodies which are variable in shape from oval to angular. Some species are deep bodied and triangular in shape, resembling somewhat the genus *Heniochus* of the family Chaetodontidae. The name armorhead comes from the peculiar characteristic of these fishes of having the head almost completely encased in rough bony plates, sometimes provided with horn-like protuberances. There is a single dorsal fin provided with anywhere from 4 to 14 spines. The spiny portion of the dorsal fin is quite different from species to species and varies from young to adult. The spines may be graduated in size, the last quite long, normal sized, or much elongated compared to the rayed portion. There are about 2-5 anal fin spines. The scales are small and rough, fused ventrally in some species. The snout may be normal or in many species produced. The mouth is small, and the jaws contain bands of small teeth. Palatine bones are without teeth, but the vomer may have small teeth. Small barbels or barbel-like processes may possibly be present on the chin. The pectoral and pelvic fins of the deep-bodied forms are usually elongate.

This family was formerly known as Histiopteridae and may still be referred to by that name in some publications, but in 1963 Follett and Dempster showed that Pentacerotidae is the proper name for this group.

Few genera are recognized. *Histiopterus*, *Zanclistius*, and *Pentaceros* are perhaps the best known, with *Paristiopterus* and *Pentaceropsis* completing the family. Only about a dozen species are known. *Histiopterus acutirostris* (or as it is sometimes called, *Evistias acutirostris*) is a fairly large species reaching a size of about 600 mm in length and is one of the deep bodied forms. *Pentaceros japonicus* (also known under the name *Quinquarius japonicus*) is more normally shaped. *Histiopterus* and *Pentaceros* are placed in separate subfamilies of the pentacerotids.

180. *Pentaceros japonicus* (Steindachner and Doderlein). Distributed from the northern part of the East China Sea, particularly around southern Japan and Korea. Photo by Dr. Shih-chieh Shen. Taiwan. (110.2 mm standard length)

181. *Pentaceros japonicus* (Steindachner and Doderlein). The bones of the head of fishes in this family are rugose, as can be seen in this species and its close relative *Pentaceros richardsoni* Smith (insert).

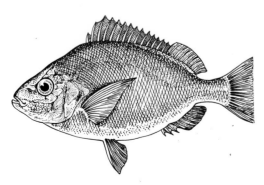

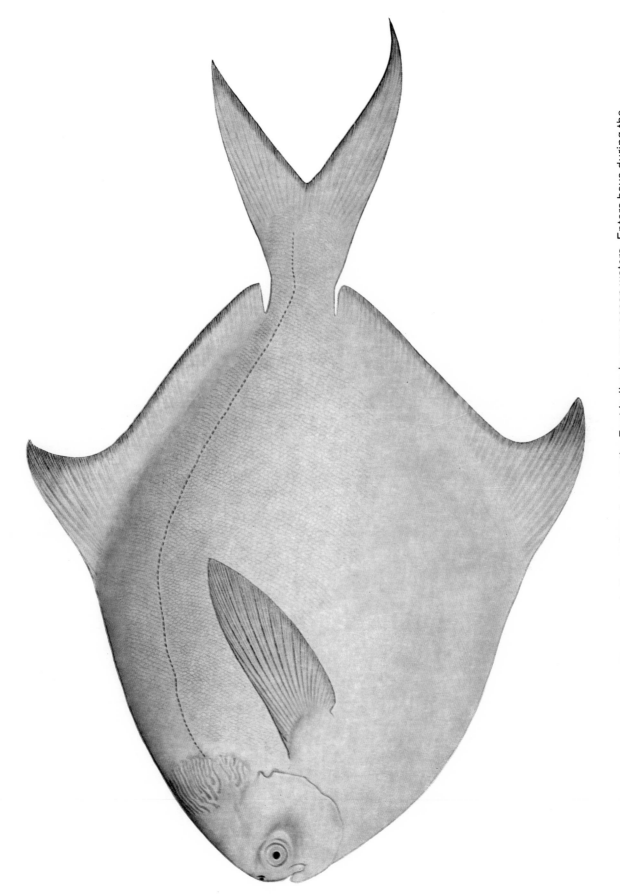

182. *Pampus argenteus* (Euphrasen). Occurs from Japan to the East Indies in open ocean waters. Enters bays during the spawning season. Illustration by Tomita.

Family STROMATEIDAE
BUTTERFISHES AND POMFRETS

The classification of these fishes seems to be in question. According to the classification system by Greenwood, et. al., there are four separate families, Stromateidae, Nomeidae, Centrolophidae, and Tetragonuridae in the suborder Stromateoidei. Since then the Ariommidae and Amarsipidae have been added by Haedrich. A second system, used in the American Fisheries Society Special Publication #6 by Bailey, et. al., places all five families (the Amarsipidae is extralimital) in the family Stromateidae and relegates the families to subfamily status. There seems then to be basic agreement as to the divisions of the group but not the level. Certainly these fishes are closely related and share a number of anatomical characteristics, perhaps the most distinctive one being the presence of an esophageal pouch which is provided with ridges, papillae, and in some cases, even teeth. TheAmarsipidae lacks this character and probably should retain its family status regardless of the others.

The stromateids (using the name in the narrow sense) are deep bodied fishes with a single long dorsal fin which is not preceded by stout spines, although there may be some blade-like spines protruding in front of the fin in *Peprilus* and *Pampus*. The anal fin is long and resembles the dorsal fin. The pelvic fins are absent in the adults and only rarely present in the young. Usually about 30-50 rays are present in the dorsal and anal fins, which are similar in shape. The caudal fin is forked and the dorsal and anal fins are higher anteriorly, falcate in many species. Three genera were recognized by Haedrich: *Peprilus*, which is only found around the coastal Americas; *Stromateus*, from the Atlantic and eastern Pacific; and *Pampus*, which occurs from Japan to the Indian Ocean.

In the genus *Pampus* the pelvic fins are absent in both adults and young. They also have the interopercles and subopercles broadly attached to the isthmus. *Pampus*

argenteus, which occurs in our area of coverage, is known from Japan to the Iranian Gulf. It has 10 spines preceding the dorsal fin and 7 preceding the anal fin, but they are covered with flesh in the adults. The caudal fin is forked and has the lower lobe longer. This species spawns in the Japanese area around June when it moves into the bays from the open ocean waters. They are used as food, being relatively common and of good taste, and are roasted with sauce in Japan. It grows to a size of about 600 mm in length. The closely related *P. chinensis* is known from China to India and is distinguished by having no spines preceding the dorsal and anal fins. A third species found in the waters of China, Korea, and Japan is very close to *P. argenteus* but differs in gill raker count.

The centrolophids (family Centrolophidae), which resemble the stromateids in some ways, also have a single dorsal fin but preceded by up to nine spines. In addition pelvic fins are always present. The anal fin has fewer fin rays than the stromateids, usually about 15-30. The dorsal and anal fins may be higher anteriorly, but never falcate, and may resemble each other in shape but not size, the anal having a shorter base than the dorsal. The centrolophids are elongate, rather than deep bodied, and compressed. They are pelagic fishes and the young are known to shelter in or around floating jetsom. They also find refuge among the tentacles of jellyfish. Six genera were recognized by Haedrich: *Centrolophus, Icichthys, Schedophilus, Hyperoglyphe, Seriolella,* and *Psenopsis. Icichthys* occurs in the northern Pacific but extends as far south as Japan (*I. lockingtoni*), *Schedophilus* has a species which reaches from the East Indies to China (*S. maculatus*), *Hyperoglyphe* has one around southern Japan which may reach Taiwan (*H. japonica*), and *Psenopsis* has a representative in Southeast Asia (*P. anomala*). The other genera are not known from Taiwan or the surrounding waters.

183. *Psenes indicus* (Day). The low number of anal fin rays distinguishes this Indian Ocean species from the closely related form below. Illustration by Arita.

184. *Psenes pellucidus* (Lutken). This species may be called by some scientists *Papyrichthys pellucidus* or *Icticus pellucidus*. A juvenile is shown in Pacific Marine Fishes Book 2, p. 419. Photo by Dr. Shih-chieh Shen. Bi-Tsian, southern tip of Taiwan. (53.4 mm standard length)

185. *Pempheris japonica* Doderlein. Sweeps usually are found in large schools and are silvery or red in color. The related *Parapriacanthus ransonneti* Steindachner (insert) is light red and occurs from Japan and Korea to the Marshall Islands. Illustration by Tomita.

186. *Pempheris oualensis* Cuvier. This silvery species grows to a length of about 7 inches. Photo by Dr. Shih-chieh Shen. Taiwan. (119 mm standard length)

187. *Pempheris klunzingeri* McCulloch. Most pempherids have this typical shape and must be distinguished by fin ray counts or other means. Illustration by Kumada. (about 160 mm)

188.
Anthias squammipinnis
(Peters). The yellowish
phase of this species.
The elongate dorsal ray
indicates this is
probably a male. Photo
by Dr. Shih-chieh Shen.
Taiwan. (85.8 mm
standard length)

189.
Anthias squammipinnis
(Peters). The reddish
phase of the same
species. Also a male.
Photo by Dr. Shih-chieh
Shen. Taiwan. (88.6 mm
standard length)

190.   *Percanthias japonicus* (Franz). Gold and red colors predominate in the *Anthias*-type fishes. Except for the above species and one or two more, few are
ever offered for sale. Illustration by Kumada. (about 19 cm)

191. *Sacura margaritacea* (Hilgendorf). The male (above) is easily distinguished from the female (below) of this species. (Photos are included in Pacific Marine Fishes Book 1, p. 238.) Illustrations by Tomita.

192. *Sayonara satsumae* Jordan and Seale. This species was discovered in Japanese
      waters in 1906. It is doubtful that its range extends as far south as Taiwan. Illus-
      tration by Tomita.

193. *Chelidoperca hirundinacea* (Valenciennes). This species may be the same as *Chelidoperca margaritifera*
      Weber. The combined range would be at least from Japan to New Guinea. Illustration by Tomita.

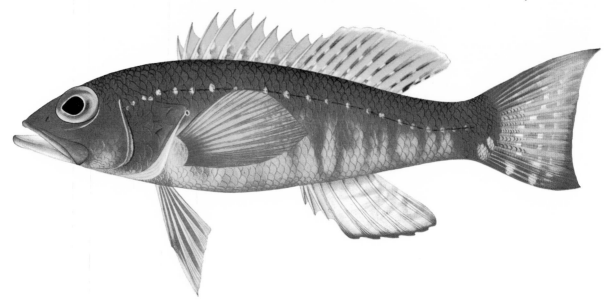

194. *Grammistes sexlineatus* (Thunberg). One of the most popular serranids is this golden-striped grouper. Photo by Dr. Shih-chieh Shen. Taiwan. (Upper fish 115 mm standard length, lower fish 79 mm standard length)

195. *Grammistes sexlineatus* (Thunberg). The reddish anterior dorsal spines and fewer stripes led to the description of a subspecies, *G. s. proerythraeus*. However, these may just be juvenile characteristics. Photo by K.H. Choo. Taiwan.

196. *Diploprion bifasciatum* Cuvier. The juvenile (insert) of this species has elongate filaments extending from the anterior dorsal fin spines. Illustration by Tomita. Indo-Pacific.

197. *Diploprion bifasciatum* Cuvier. The extent of the black banding varies. This one has less black than the one illustrated on the opposite page. Photo by Dr. Shih-chieh Shen. Hong-Loo-Chun, Pescadore Islands. (187.2 mm standard length)

198. *Doderleinia berycoides* (Hilgendorf). This serranid is rather common in deeper water. It attains a length of about 50 cm. Illustration by Arita. Southern Japan and Korea.

199. *Malakichthys wakiyai* Jordan and Hubbs. Another species which is rather common but is restricted to deeper water. It is found around Japan, though its close relative, *M. griseus*, extends south to China and the Philippines. This latter species has fewer pored scales in the lateral line. Illustration by Arita.

200 & 201.   *Variola louti* (Forskal). The upper fish has a somewhat different color pattern than the one below. This species attains a length of about 30 inches. Photos by Dr. Shih-chieh Shen. Ma-Kung, Pescadore Islands. (Upper specimen 116 mm standard length; lower specimen 119 mm standard length)

202. *Plectropomus leopardus* (Lacepede). Individuals of about 2 feet in length are most common although this species attains 3 feet in length. Photo by Dr. Shih-chieh Shen. Ma-Kung, Pescadore Islands. (357 mm standard length)

203. *Plectropomus maculatus* (Bloch). The color of this species is highly variable, ranging from this brown color to a reddish or pink hue. Photo by Dr. Shih-chieh Shen. Ma-Kung, Pescadore Islands. (148 mm standard length)

204. *Plectropomus maculatus* (Bloch). The dark edged blue spots are one of the identifying features of this species. Reaches a length of over 3 feet and a weight of 50 pounds or more. Photo by Dr. Shih-chieh Shen. Taiwan. (125 mm standard length)

205. *Plectropomus maculatus* (Bloch). Banded phase. The blue spots are still visible on some parts of the body. Photo by Dr. Shih-chieh Shen. Wan-Li-Tung, southern tip of Taiwan. (147 mm standard length)

206. *Stereolepis ischinagi* (Hilgendorf). Normally deeper water inhabitant (400-500 meters deep) found around rocks. Attains a length of 2 meters. Illustration by Arita. Southern Japan and Korea.

207. *Coreoperca kawamebari* (Temminck and Schlegel). This genus has at times been synonymized with *Siniperca*. Illustration by Arita.

208. *Lates calcarifer* (Bloch). A sea bass of the family Centropomidae. The barramundi and others in the family are known for their eyes, which seem to glow at night. *L. calcarifer* is reported to have glowing pink eyes at night. Illustration by Kumada. Indo-Pacific.

209. *Cephalopholis boenack* (Bloch). The inside of the mouth and the gill cavity is reported to be orange. Photo by Dr. Shih-chieh Shen. Taiwan. (179 mm standard length)

210. *Cephalopholis argus* Bloch and Schneider. Widespread in the Indo-Pacific. Attains a length of 1½ feet. Photo by K.H. Choo. Taiwan.

211. *Cephalopholis pachycentron* (Valenciennes). The pattern of this fish may show about eight vertical bands. Photo by Dr. Shih-chieh Shen. Toi-Chi, northeastern part of Taiwan. (432.7 mm standard length)

212. *Epinephelus fasciatus* (Forskal). Named black-tip grouper in reference to the edge of the dorsal fin. Grows to more than a foot in length. Photo by Dr. Shih-chieh Shen. Taiwan. (152 mm standard length)

213. *Cephalopholis aurantius* (Valenciennes). A coral reef grouper that reaches 14 inches in length. Illustration by Kumada.

214. *Cephalopholis urodelus* (Bloch and Schneider). An excellent food fish found in numbers off Taiwan at about 100-200 feet depth. Indo-Pacific. Photo by Dr. Shih-chieh Shen. Taiwan. (172 mm standard length)

215. *Cephalopholis urodelus* (Bloch and Schneider). Notice the difference in color between this individual and the one above. Photo by Dr. Shih-chieh Shen. Taiwan. (125 mm standard length)

216. *Epinephelus fasciatus* (Forskal). The intensity of color can be changed drastically from a near white to this color. Photo by Dr. Shih-chieh Shen. Taiwan. 136 mm standard length)

217.
*Epinephelus
fasciatomaculatus*
(Peters). Rather
restricted in its range
and known only from the
Philippines to south
China and Taiwan.
Photo by Dr. Shih-chieh
Shen. Taiwan. (168 mm
standard length)

218.   *Epinephelus awoara* (Temminck and Schlegel). A market species found around 100 feet deep. Known only
from China and Japan. Photo by Dr. Shih-chieh Shen. Tang-Shui, northern part of Taiwan. (255 mm standard length)

219. *Epinephelus fasciatomaculatus* (Peters). A younger specimen of the rock grouper. It feeds on worms, snails, and small crustaceans. Photo by Dr. Shih-chieh Shen. Taiwan. (43 mm standard length)

220. *Epinephelus rhyncholepis* (Bleeker). The pattern around the chest and behind the mouth is distinctive. Photo by Dr. Shih-chieh Shen. Ma-Kung, Pescadore Islands. (195 mm standard length)

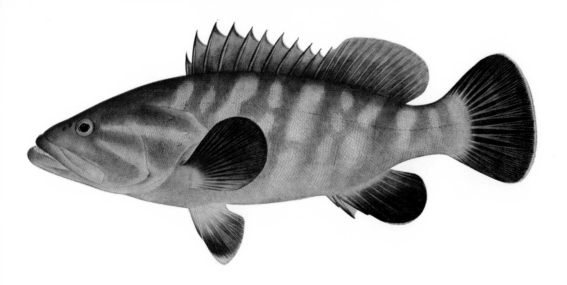

221.
Epinephelus moara
(Temminck and
Schlegel). Adults are
deeper water fishes but
the young are found in
tide-pools. Known from
Japan, Korea and China
to the Palau Islands.
Illustration by Tomita.

222.
Epinephelus akaara
(Temminck and
Schlegel).
Normally a foot in length
but can get to twice that
large. Known only from
the areas of China and
Japan. Illustration by
Arita.

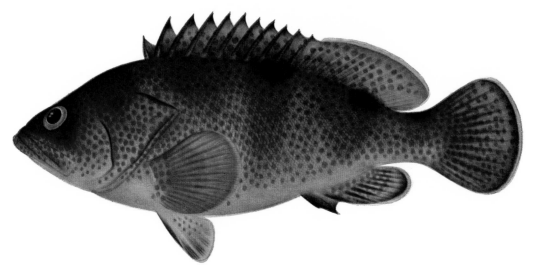

223.
Epinephelus fario
(Thunberg). A common
Indo-Pacific grouper
found in intertidal
regions and around
rocks where seaweed is
present. Illustration by
Tomita.

224. *Epinephelus septemfasciatus* (Thunberg). This grouper is recorded from the Pacific, Indian and Atlantic Oceans. Shallow water species that spawns in May in Japan. Illustration by Tomita.

225. *Epinephelus epistictus* (Temminck and Schlegel). This species is easily identified by its color and pattern. China and Japan. Illustration by Arita.

226. *Epinephelus cometae* Tanaka. Another grouper that is quite easily identified by its pattern. Illustration by Arita.

227.
Epinephelus tauvina
(Forskal). The estuary
grouper is widespread
throughout the Indo-
Pacific area and is
relatively abundant in
the Taiwan region from
inshore bays and
estuaries to the offshore
commercial fishing
grounds. Photo by Dr.
Shih-chieh Shen.
Taiwan. (108.4 mm
standard length)

228.
Epinephelus sp. This
fish is very much like
E. tukula Morgans, but
that species is known
only from the western
Indian Ocean. Photo by
Dr. Shih-chieh Shen.
Taiwan. (385 mm
standard length)

229.
Epinephelus merra
Bloch. The common
names honeycomb
grouper and wire-netting
grouper are descriptive
of the pattern that can
be seen on the side and
fins of this fish. Photo
by Dr. Shih-chieh Shen.
Taiwan. (145 mm
standard length)

230. *Epinephelus tauvina* (Forskal). This and the following two photos represent stages in the development of the color pattern of this grouper. A larger fish is shown in photo #227. Photo by Dr. Shih-chieh Shen. Taiwan. (55 mm standard length)

231. *Epinephelus tauvina* (Forskal). The spotting on this species can be anywhere from orange-red to olive-black. Photo by Dr. Shih-chieh Shen. Taiwan. (66.4 mm standard length)

232. *Epinephelus tauvina* (Forskal). These fishes are still babies when it is realized that full size may mean a length of 7 feet and a weight of 500 pounds. Photo by Dr. Shih-chieh Shen. Taiwan.

1245

233. *Epinephelus amblycephalus* (Bleeker). This species is recognized by the black spots edging the dark bands. Illustration by Tomita.

234. *Epinephelus caeruleopunctatus* (Bloch). The white margins on the fins and the dark edging to the white spots are characteristics used to identify this young fish. Photo by Dr. Shih-chieh Shen. Taiwan. (54.8 mm standard length)

235. *Epinephelus macrospilus* (Bleeker). Known from the western Pacific Ocean. It was originally discovered in the East Indies. Photo by Dr. Shih-chieh Shen. Taiwan. (157 mm standard length)

236. *Epinephelus caeruleopunctatus* (Bloch). With age the dark edging to the white spots becomes diffuse and eventually disappears. Photo by Dr. Shih-chieh Shen. Taiwan. (72.4 mm standard length)

237. *Epinephelus caeruleopunctatus* (Bloch). This larger fish is still small compared to the 2½ foot adult stage. Photo by Dr. Shih-chieh Shen. Taiwan.

238.
Epinephelus hexagonatus (Bloch and Schneider). This and the following two photos show the hexagon grouper in its growth stages. The largest specimen is first. Photo by Dr. Shih-chieh Shen. Taiwan. (168 mm standard length)

239.
Epinephelus hexagonatus (Bloch and Schneider). This species has at times been synonymized with *E. merra*. Here we consider them separate species. Photo by Dr. Shih-chieh Shen. Taiwan. (147 mm standard length)

240.
Epinephelus hexagonatus (Bloch and Schneider). Juvenile. This grouper is very colorful and would do well in captivity. Groupers hide much of the time and would have to be coaxed out into the open with food for viewing. Photo by Dr. Shih-chieh Shen. Taiwan. (53.5 mm standard length)

241. *Epinephelus megachir* (Richardson). Like many other groupers, the natural diet consists of fishes, crustaceans, and marine worms. Substitutes for this carnivorous diet are easily available as frozen packaged food. Photo by Dr. Shih-chieh Shen. Taiwan. (152.5 mm standard length)

242. *Epinephelus megachir* (Richardson). This grouper reaches a length of almost two feet, but more commonly one-foot-long specimens are encountered. Photo by Dr. Shih-chieh Shen. Taiwan. (89 mm standard length)

243. *Epinephelus fario* (Thunberg). A wide-ranging grouper found from Africa to the western Pacific. Photo by Dr. Shih-chieh Shen. Taiwan. (111 mm standard length)

1249

244. *Epinephelus fasciatus* (Forskal). Tropical waters of the Indo-Pacific region. It extends as far north as Korea in our area. Illustration by Tomita.

245. *Epinephelus megachir* (Richardson). Juveniles of aquarium size (1-2 inches) may be collected in shallow intertidal areas in the summer months. Photo by Dr. Shih-chieh Shen. Huing-Lo-Tsuin, southern tip of Taiwan. (111 mm standard length)

246. *Trisotropis dermopterus* (Temminck and Schlegel). This species is caught by trawlers over mud bottoms. Its range is restricted to China and Japan. Illustration by Tomita.

247. *Epinephelus fario* (Thunberg). The black saddle on the caudal peduncle helps identify this grouper. Photo by Dr. Shih-chieh Shen. Ma-Kung, Pescadore Islands. (122 mm standard length)

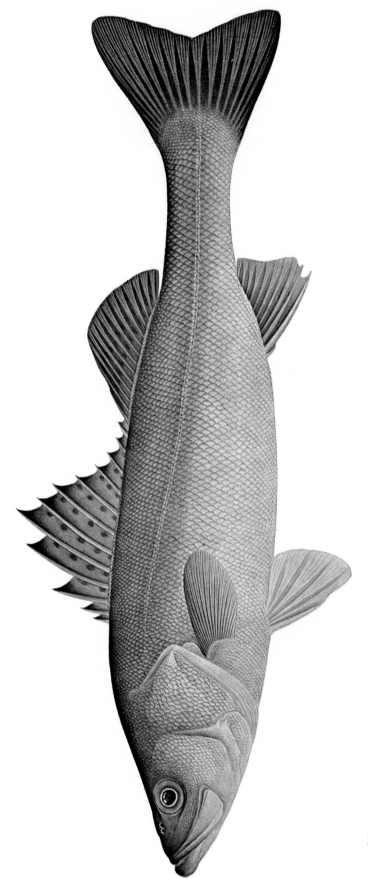

248.   *Lateolabrax japonicus* (Cuvier and Valenciennes). Reaches a length of over 1 meter. Korea and Japan to China and the Philippines. Illustration by Arita.

249. *Calloplesiops altivelis* (Steindachner). The comet is one of the more spectacularly patterned groupers. Photo by K.H. Choo. Taiwan.

250. *Calloplesiops altivelis* (Steindachner). The fins of this individual are slightly damaged but will grow back as good as new. Photo by K.H. Choo. Taiwan.

Family GLAUCOSOMIDAE
BULLSEYES

The Glaucosomidae is a small family of moderate sized fishes, mostly no larger than two feet in length. They occur in the Pacific Ocean and are best known from China and Japan to Australia.

The compressed body is oval to suborbicular and robust. The head is large and the mouth also, the latter being protractile with a prominent lower jaw. The mouth cleft is oblique, and the teeth are set in narrow bands (some canine-like teeth are present) in the jaws. The vomer and usually the palatines and tongue are provided with teeth. The ctenoid scales are small to moderate and adherent. A single dorsal fin is present, composed of about eight spines and a dozen or more rays. The soft part of the fin is higher than the spinous part, and in one species, *Glaucosoma magnificus*, some of the rays are prolonged into filaments. The anal fin has three spines and about 12 soft rays and is similar to the soft portion of the dorsal fin. The pectoral fins are short, the caudal fin truncate, and the pelvic fins are thoracic in position.

Several species have been reported in the only(?) genus in the family, *Glaucosoma. Glaucosoma fauveli*, which occurs from Japan to China and the Philippines, is said to inhabit rather deep waters and is considered rare. It is not a good eating fish, although it is utilized for fish cakes in

251. *Glaucosoma magnificus* Ogilby. This related form from Australian waters has elongate filaments on the non-paired fins. Illustration by Kumada.

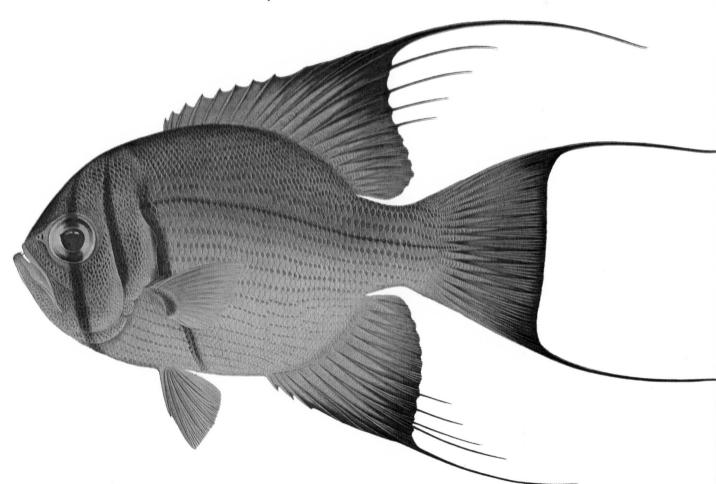

Japan along with other fishes. It reaches a size of about 300 mm. The related species *G. hebraicum* is more widely distributed, from Japan to Australia, and is distinguishable from *fauveli* by the lateral line scale count (50 in *hebraicum* and 60 in *fauveli*). The Australian species *G. scapulare* is an important food fish there and is usually taken around sunken reefs. It grows to two feet in length. *Glaucosoma magnificus*, the threadfin bullseye, is also from Australian waters and can easily be recognized by the filaments extending from the dorsal and anal fins and the upper and lower edges of the caudal fin.

252. *Glaucosoma fauveli* Sauvage. The young individuals have fewer but heavier stripes. Illustration by Tomita.

253. *Glaucosoma fauveli* Sauvage. A rare fish inhabiting rather deep waters. Known from Japan to China and the Philippines. Photo by Dr. Shih-chieh Shen. Ma-Kung, Pescadore Islands.

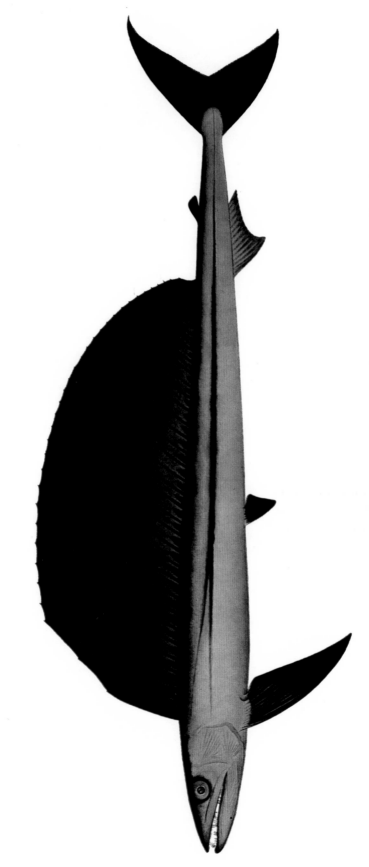

254. *Alepisaurus borealis* (Gill). Another rare deep water fish. It reaches a size of about 3 meters and occurs in the tropical and temperate Pacific. Illustration by Tomita.

Family ALEPISAURIDAE
LANCETFISHES

The family Alepisauridae belongs to a group of fishes, suborder Myctophoidei, which includes many of the "deep-sea" fishes as well as the synodontids or lizard-fishes which inhabit relatively shallow waters.

The lancetfishes are elongate, slightly compressed fishes with a large, sail-like dorsal fin and a large mouth with wicked looking fang-like teeth. The dorsal fin is high and long, resembling in some ways that of the sailfishes. The rays that make up this fin are usually slender, simple, and able to be folded back into a groove, making the fin invisible when depressed. An adipose fin is present. The caudal fin is forked, and the small pelvic fins are located back on the abdomen. The mouth cleft is wide and the teeth are long, triangular, and pointed. The body is flaccid and lacks scales. No gas bladder is present.

Lancetfishes are bathypelagic, inhabiting the deeper waters of the tropical, temperate and arctic seas of the Pacific and Atlantic Oceans. They grow to a size of about 6 feet and are ferocious predators, eating anything and everything. Scientists have capitalized on this by examining the stomach contents for deep water fishes that they could otherwise not have been able to catch. The lancetfishes are sometimes seen near the surface due to storms or gas caused by poorly digested food, and they may be caught by longline fishing.

Lancetfishes are reported to be hermaphroditic—both sexes in one individual. Perhaps this is an adaptation for a rare deep water fish that would have trouble finding a mate.

The scientific name of one of the species, *Alepisaurus ferox*, freely translated is scaleless ferocious serpent. The name seems well deserved, as the food includes such things as pelagic crustaceans, worms, molluscs, squids, coelenterates, and fishes. They in turn are fed upon by sharks, tunas, etc. They are not considered good food for human consumption.

Family ISTIOPHORIDAE
SAILFISHES, SPEARFISHES, AND MARLINS

The sailfishes, spearfishes, and marlins are well known among the world's most popular gamefishes. Of all the fish trophies that are mounted, the sailfish probably ranks number one with most anglers. Clubs and tournaments are formed for fishing these giants. Typically a bait or lure is trolled behind a fast-moving boat, the line running up through outriggers before being placed in the water. This is to help hook the fish which will attack the bait, hitting at it with its bill and then moving in on the motionless bait. The line pinned to the outrigger will pop out on the first hit, giving enough slack so that the bait lies motionless for a second or two. The sailfish will then take the bait and the angler can set the hook (if he is lucky). The hooked fish will often put on a spectacular display of leaps and gyrations as it tries to free itself from the hook. The fight may last some time, the angler having to be strapped into a swivel chair mounted on the deck of the boat. Sometimes it is a toss-up as to which will tire first, man or fish. Many sportsmen are satisfied with the fight alone and will release the fish once it is brought up next to the boat. Others who wish a trophy or want to eat the fish (it is highly prized and quite expensive), will bring it back to port.

Istiophorids are elongate and compressed, heavier anteriorly and tapering back to a slender caudal peduncle. The upper jaw bones (premaxillary and maxillary) are extended into a swordlike arrangement, which is one of the chief characteristics of this family. There are two dorsal fins, the first long and either high and sail-like (sailfishes) or high in front but fairly low the rest of its length (marlins and spearfishes). The second dorsal fin is low and short and consists of only 6-7 rays. It is situated near the posterior end of the fish, with the similar second anal fin opposite. The anterior fin consists of about 2 spines and 11-14 rays. Pectoral fins and ventral fins are elongate, the former long and falcate, the latter composed of one spine and two rays.

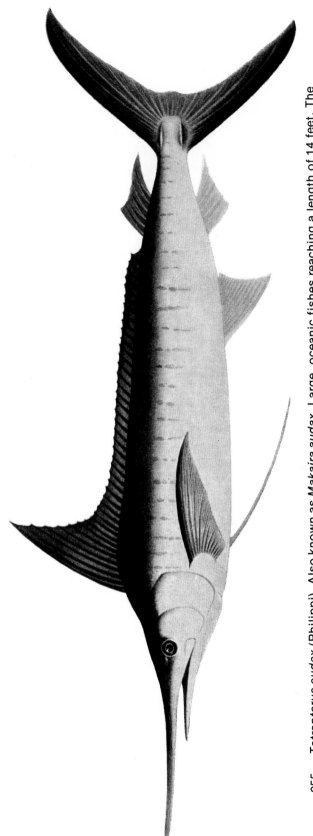

255.   *Tetrapterus audax* (Philippi). Also known as *Makaira audax*. Large, oceanic fishes reaching a length of 14 feet. The closely related species *M. indica* and *M. mazara* are shown in the inserts on page 1259. Illustrations by Tomita.

256.   *Xiphias gladius* Linnaeus. Circumtropical. This species may be found in small groups, but they keep their distance (more than 100 meters) from each other. Illustration by Tomita.

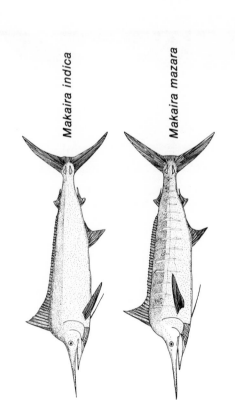

Makaira indica

Makaira mazara

257.   *Istiophorus platypterus* (Shaw and Nodder). The taxonomy of the sailfishes is still not straightened out. Illustration by Tomita.

The sailfishes and marlins are capable of fast speeds, with estimates of up to 50 miles per hour attributed to them. Their form is streamlined, starting with the long pointed spear, the fins which fold back neatly against the body into grooves, and the tapering form, ending in the powerful forked tail. This high speed enables them to catch swift mackerels and other scombroids, flyingfishes, etc. It has also led to some tales of these fish attacking small boats and penetrating the wood with their bills. There are exhibits in museums which have actual spears penetrating wood of almost two feet in thickness.

The systematics of the billfishes are not completely worked out. One difficulty of working with these fishes is that a museum cannot afford the space to keep such large specimens. The ichthyologist must go out to the field, in this instance the docks where these fishes are landed, to study them. Also being pelagic in nature, it is difficut to keep track of these fishes, and many a fisherman has sought for a long time to finally land his prized sail.

This family includes some of the largest of fishes, with weights exceeding 1,000 pounds and lengths of 14 feet or more not unusual in some species.

The sailfishes, spearfishes, and marlins should not be confused with the other billfish, the swordfish (Xiphiidae). The differences between the two families are: the swordfish has a single lateral keel on the caudal peduncle (istiophorids have two), they lack ventral fins, and the body is scaleless in adults (istiophorids have long, narrow, pointed scales imbedded in the skin).

Family CORYPHAENIDAE
DOLPHINS

The dolphins are another group of well-known fishes. They are caught trolling along "weed lines" and, once hooked, provide a battle for the angler that is not quickly forgotten. A dolphin will run, dodge, and leap continuously, trying to shake the hook (and they often succeed). When boated the dolphin will go through color changes at a rapid pace to finally settle on a green to silvery color. Usually when one dolphin is hooked several others will be taken in short succession, the other dolphin apparently keeping close to the hooked animal for some reason. Aside from being a game fish, dolphin flesh is of excellent flavor and commands relatively high prices in markets and restaurants.

The dolphins are elongate, compressed, and taper to a narrow caudal peduncle. The adult male common dolphin has the frontal part of the head enlarged, forming a very blunt and squarish profile. These fishes are often called bull dolphin. The scales are small and imbedded in the skin. There is a long dorsal fin, composed of many rays (50-70), extending from the head to the tail base. The anal fin is shorter and also lacks spines. The pectoral fins are falcate, the pelvics long, and the caudal fin forked. Bands of sharp teeth are present in the jaws and some patches of villiform teeth may be found on the tongue. Teeth are also present on vomer and palatines.

Two species are known, *Coryphaena hippurus* and *C. equiselis*. Both are widespread in distribution in tropical and temperate waters. They are swift fishes feeding on a variety of other fishes, including flyingfishes, and on various pelagic invertebrates.

Coryphaena hippurus, the common dolphin, grows fairly large, attaining a size of five feet or more and a weight of more than sixty pounds. The smaller pompano dolphin (*C. equiselis*) grows to only 30 inches and matures at about half that size; it is comparatively rare.

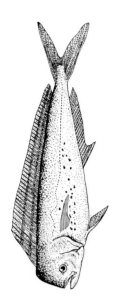

Bull dolphin, adult male of *C. hippurus*.

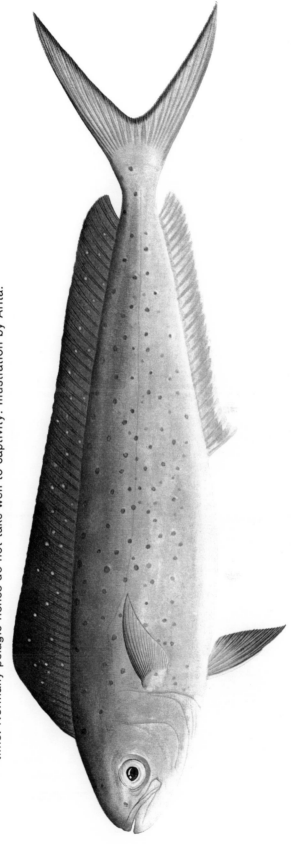

258.   *Coryphaena hippurus* (Linnaeus). The young of this popular gamefish have been kept in aquaria for short periods of time. Normally pelagic fishes do not take well to captivity. Illustration by Arita.

259. *Pseudochromis melanotaenia* Bleeker. Known mostly from the East Indies but extends northward to Taiwan. Photo by Dr. Shih-chieh Shen. Taiwan. (39 mm standard length)

260. *Labracinus cyclophthalmus* (Muller and Troschel). Female? A very variable species which exhibits sexual dimorphism. Because of this the taxonomy is still unsettled. Photo by Dr. Shih-chieh Shen. Ma-Kung, Pescadore Islands. (101 mm standard length)

261. *Labracinus cyclophthalmus* (Muller and Troschel). The dark blotch in the middle of the dorsal fin may indicate that this is a male. Photo by Dr. Shih-chieh Shen. Ma-Kung, Pescadore Islands. (124 mm standard length)

262. *Labracinus cyclophthalmus* (Muller and Troschel). Although similar to the other specimens on these pages, there is no dorsal fin blotch nor blackish tail. Photo by K.H. Choo. Taiwan.

263. *Pseudochromis aureus* Seale. This species was originally discovered in the Philippine Islands. Photo by K.H. Choo. Taiwan.

264. *Pseudochromis melanotaenia* Bleeker. Pseudochro mids are occasionally offered for sale to the marir aquarist. This one would be included in a Philippir shipment. Photo by K.H. Choo. Taiwan.

265. *Pseudochromis cyanotaenia* Bleeker. Like their relatives the groupers, pseudochromids remain on or near the bottom or resting on some tank decoration like this one. Photo by K.H. Choo. Taiwan.

Family **LOBOTIDAE**
TRIPLETAILS

The family Lobotidae includes fishes that are favorites among the fresh water aquarists, genus *Datnioides*. It also includes the tripletail familiar to marine aquarists, *Lobotes surinamensis*. With two or three species of *Datnioides* (*Datnioides quadrifasciatus, D. microlepis* and *D. campbelli*), and a similar number of *Lobotes* (*Lobotes surinamensis* and *L. pacificus*), this family is quite small. The species themselves may grow quite large, *Lobotes surinamensis* attaining a length of some 40 inches and a weight of about 30 pounds.

Tripletails are perch-like, compressed fishes with a single dorsal fin slightly notched between spinous and soft portions. The rounded caudal fin together with the extended rounded dorsal and anal fins create the appearance that gives them their common name—tripletails. The ventral fins are thoracic, and there is a scaly axillary process present. The mouth is moderate, slightly protractile, the jaws with an outer row of enlarged conical teeth and inner narrow bands of small pointed teeth. No teeth are present on the palate.

Lobotids as a group inhabit inshore waters (marine) as well as brackish and pure fresh water. Most of them can be found in the tropical Indo-Pacific, and one species, *Lobotes surinamensis*, is very widely distributed in the Indo-Pacific and occurs in the Atlantic Ocean as well. The young fishes, of a size of 2-4 inches or so, mimic floating leaves, an action aided by their flattened leaf-like shape. They float at the surface among leaves and other debris and are very hard to spot. Once detected they look like they are dead, and if prodded will dart away quickly startling the observer. It is a simple matter to net one of these as they rely on their camouflage to a great extent and do not move unless almost touched. The larger fishes may be caught on hook and line and are considered quite a game fish. They are also good eating.

266. *Lobotes surinamensis* (Bloch). The tripletail is normally found in coastal and brackish waters. Circumtropical. Illustration by Tomita.

Family POMATOMIDAE
BLUEFISH

The bluefish, *Pomatomus saltatrix*, is the only species included in this family. It has an extremely wide range, occurring in tropical and temperate waters around the world (but not in the eastern and central Pacific Ocean). Wherever it is found it has the reputation of being ferocious or bloodthirsty, and in one case was even mentioned as reminding the writer of the South American piranha. This fast moving schooling fish will attack a school of mullet, menhaden, or other fish, and upon satisfying its hunger will continue to kill simply for pure destructiveness. Young bluefish, called snappers or tailors, hunt their prey in schools and apparently enjoy the excess killing as much as the adults. Although the name snappers is applied to these juvenile fishes, there is no connection with the true snappers, family Lutjanidae.

These fast, powerful swimmers are game fish and provide the angler with many hours of hard fishing as a school moves through his area. They are excellent eating fish, as both of us can testify, especially after having caught them ourselves.

The body is elongate, compressed, and streamlined in appearance, and is covered with moderate size scales. The head is large, with an oblique, wide mouth, and the jaws are provided with a single row of strong, sharp teeth and an inner series of small depressible teeth in the upper jaw. The vomer, palatines, and tongue have villiform teeth. The first dorsal fin is composed of seven to eight small spines that are depressible into a groove (for streamlining). The second dorsal fin and the anal fin are long, densely scaled, and of about the same size and shape. There are one or two anal fin spines which are small and may be imbedded in the skin.

Bluefish may reach a length of four feet and a weight of over 30 pounds. Considering the fighting ability of these fishes, even a much smaller fish can provide a battle that is memorable.

267. *Pomatomus saltatrix* (Linnaeus). Bluefish. This species has been described as a ferocious carnivore, killing in excess of their needs. It is a well known food and game fish around the world. Illustration by Tomita.

268 & 269. *Gaterin albovittatus* (Ruppell). Only the upper stripes remain as the fish grows to adulthood (see PMF Book 2, p. 348). Photos by K.H. Choo. Taiwan.

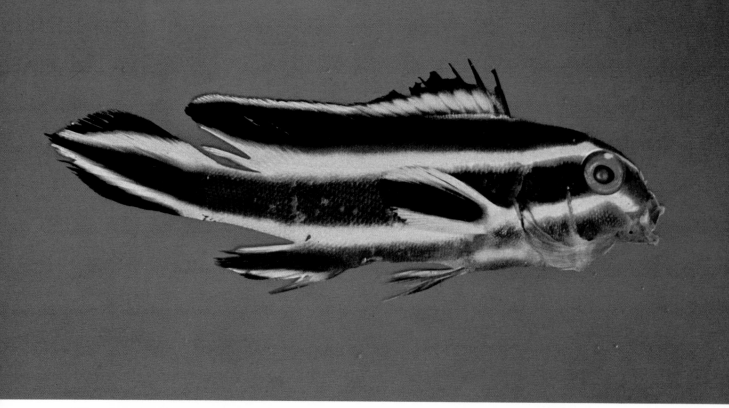

270. *Gaterin albovittatus* (Ruppell). An Indo-Pacific species reaching 8 inches in length. Photo by Dr. Shih-chieh Shen. Ao-Luan-bi, southern tip of Taiwan. (39 mm standard length)

271. *Spilotichthys pictus* (Thunberg). Juvenile. This species has also been called *Diagramma pictum*. Photo by Dr. Shih-chieh Shen. Houng-Lo-Tsiun, southern tip of Taiwan. (48.4 mm standard length)

272. *Gaterin flavomaculatus* (Ehrenberg). One of the lesser known sweetlips. Indo-Pacific in distribution. Photo by Dr. Shih-chieh Shen. Tam-Shui, northern Taiwan. (290 mm standard length)

273. *Gaterin chaetodonoides* (Lacepede). Juvenile. A shallow water coastal fish that attains a length of about 1½ feet. Photo by K.H. Choo. Taiwan.

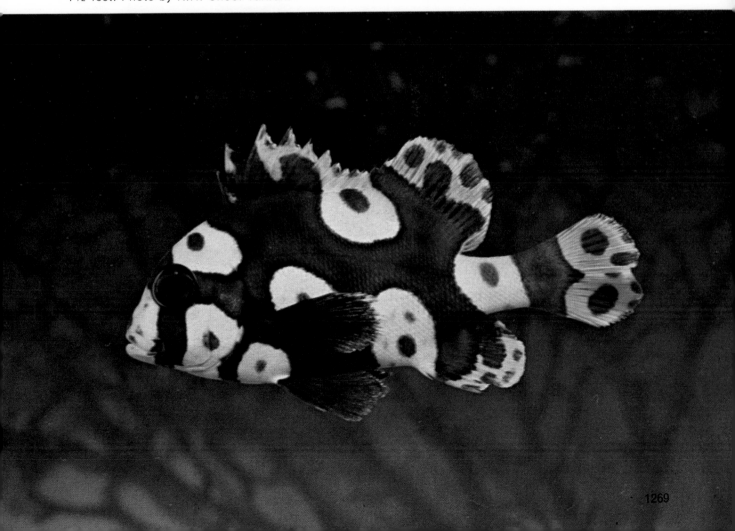

274.
Gaterin sp. ? The small mouth makes inclusion in this genus probable. Photo by Dr. Shih-chieh Shen. Taiwan. (112 mm standard length)

275.
Spilotichthys pictus (Thunberg). This sub-adult is very close to an adult in coloration. This species grows to 1½ feet. Photo by Dr. Shih-chieh Shen. Taiwan. (179 mm standard length)

276.
Spilotichthys pictus (Thunberg). A younger individual of the same species but showing more of the juvenile pattern. Photo by Dr. Shih-chieh Shen. Taiwan. (109 mm standard length)

277. *Gaterin orientalis* (Bloch). Note the difference between the fin patterns of this specimen and the two below. Photo by Dr. Shih-chieh Shen. Taiwan. (143 mm standard length)

278. *Gaterin orientalis* (Bloch). This older specimen has a more spotted fin pattern. Photo by Dr. Shih-chieh Shen. Taiwan. (185 mm standard length)

279. *Gaterin orientalis* (Bloch). This species attains a length of 16 inches. At this length additional lines are seen ventrally. Photo by Dr. Shih-chieh Shen. Taiwan. (279 mm standard length)

280. *Pseudopristopoma nigra* (Cuvier). The brown sweetlips inhabits shallow coastal waters. Grows to 2 feet. Photo by Dr. Shih-chieh Shen. Taiwan. (113.5 mm standard length)

281. *Gaterin orientalis* (Bloch). Encountered on the reefs of the Indo-Pacific region. Photo by Dr. Shih-chieh Shen. Pai-Sha, southern tip of Taiwan. (184 mm standard length)

282. *Gaterin picus* (Cuvier and Valenciennes). The juveniles are very close to those of *Gaterin orientalis*. The dorsal fin count helps separate them. Photo by K.H. Choo. Taiwan.

283. *Gaterin picus* (Cuvier and Valenciennes). The swimming motions of these juveniles may almost be called serpentine or undulating. Photo by K.H. Choo. Taiwan.

284. *Gaterin picus* (Cuvier and Valenciennes). The contrast between *G. picus* and *G. orientalis* (opposite) juveniles can be seen here. Note the dark snout tip in *G. orientalis*. Photo by Dr. Shih-chieh Shen. Kee-Lung, northern tip of Taiwan. (88 mm standard length)

285. *Gaterin orientalis* (Bloch). Post-juvenile form showing changing color pattern. Photo by K.H. Choo. Taiwan.

286.	*Gaterin orientalis* (Bloch). Juvenile. Additional differentiating characteristics between *G. orientalis* and *G. picus* are the dark anal and pectoral fins of this species. Photo by Dr. Shih-chieh Shen. Mo-Bi-Tau, northern tip of Taiwan. (35.2 mm standard length)

287.	*Gaterin orientalis* (Bloch). A later stage than the individual opposite. The breaking up of the pattern into stripes is much more evident. Photo by K.H. Choo. Taiwan.

288. *Lutjanus russelli* (Bleeker). The adults of this snapper may be found on coral reefs. Juveniles may be collected more inshore. Illustration by Kumada.

289. *Macolor niger* (Forskal). Note how similar the color pattern of this snapper is to some of the gaterins on the previous pages. Photo by K.H. Choo. Taiwan.

290. *Lutjanus gibbus* (Forskal). Widespread in the tropical waters of the Indo-Pacific region. Two color phases. Illustrations by Arita. (upper fish about 290 mm, lower fish 220 mm standard length)

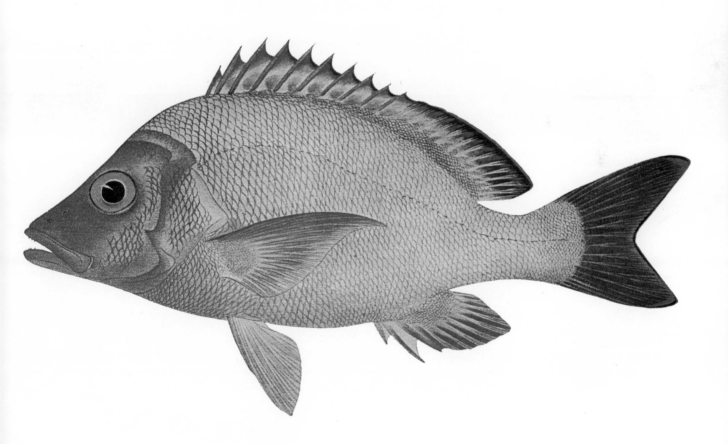

291.   *Lutjanus flavipes* (Valenciennes). Known from Melanesia and the East Indies to Africa. Illustration by To-mita.

292.   *Lutjanus quinquelineatus* (Bloch). Often confused with *L. kasmira* but has been called distinct, partially due to the striping on the head. Photo by Dr. Shih-chieh Shen. Hing-Chuen, southern tip of Taiwan. (200 mm standard length)

293. *Lutjanus kasmira* (Forskal). Attains a length of about 15 inches. One of the more attractive snappers. Photo by Dr. Shih-chieh Shen. Taiwan. (163 mm standard length)

294. *Lutjanus carponotatus* (Richardson). A multi-striped snapper that occurs from Fiji and the East Indies to the northern coast of Australia. Illustration by Kumada.

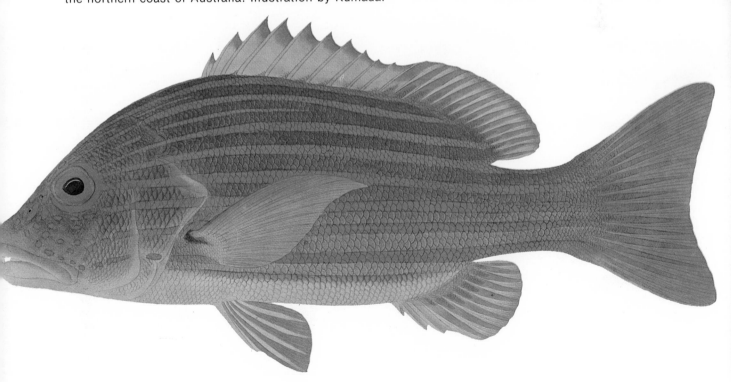

295.
Lutjanus rivulatus
(Cuvier). Indo-Pacific.
Juveniles have the white
spot bordered with
black. Photo by Dr.
Shih-chieh Shen.
Taiwan. (91 mm
standard length)

296.
Lutjanus rivulatus
(Cuvier). Attains a
length of about 2 feet.
The white spot may
disappear with age.
Photo by Dr. Shih-chieh
Shen. Taiwan. (196 mm
standard length)

297.
Lutjanus argenti-
maculatus (Forskal).
The mangrove snapper
occurs along coastal
areas, often among
mangroves, and even
enters brackish waters
of estuaries. Photo by
Dr. Shih-chieh Shen.
Taiwan. (98 mm
standard length)

298. *Lutjanus semicinctus* Quoy and Gaimard. The characteristic seven vertical bands are barely visible in this specimen. The horizontal stripes are a juvenile character. Photo by Dr. Shih-chieh Shen. Hong-Loo-Chun, Pescadore Islands. (82 mm standard length)

299. *Lutjanus semicinctus* Quoy and Gaimard. The adult pattern is quite distinct from the juvenile above. Illustration by Arita.

300. *Lutjanus vaigiensis* (Quoy and Gaimard). The dusky red margin of the dorsal fin is a characteristic of *L. vaigiensis*. Photo by Dr. Shih-chieh Shen. Hong-Loo-Chun, Pescadore Islands. (98 mm standard length)

301. *Lutjanus johni* (Bloch). The black blotch on the flank is found in several species of snapper. Photo by Dr. Shih-chieh Shen. Ma-Kung, Pescadore Islands. (162.6 mm standard length)

302. *Lutjanus janthinuropterus* (Bleeker). A coastal and coral reef snapper that attains a length of 2½ feet. Photo by Dr. Shih-chieh Shen. Taiwan. (124 mm standard length)

303. *Lutjanus janthinuropterus* (Bleeker). In this individual the yellow body stripes are more prominent. Photo by Dr. Shih-chieh Shen. Taiwan. (76 mm standard length)

304. *Lutjanus janthinuropterus* (Bleeker). A different color phase. Note the continued presence of the blackish dorsal edge and caudal fin. Photo by Dr. Shih-chieh Shen. Taiwan. (109 mm standard length)

305. *Lutjanus erythropterus* Bloch. A comparison of the adult (above) and sub-adult (below) color phases. Notice the weakening of the caudal peduncle band. Illustrations by Arita.

306. *Lutjanus erythropterus* Bloch. Young. Widely distributed from the western Pacific Ocean to the Red Sea. It has also been referred to as *L. sanguineus*. Photo by Dr. Shih-chieh Shen. Taiwan. (84 mm standard length)

307. *Lutjanus janthinuropterus* (Bleeker). Juveniles of this species have a lateral band from eye to tail base, bordered above by a pale stripe. Illustration by Tomita.

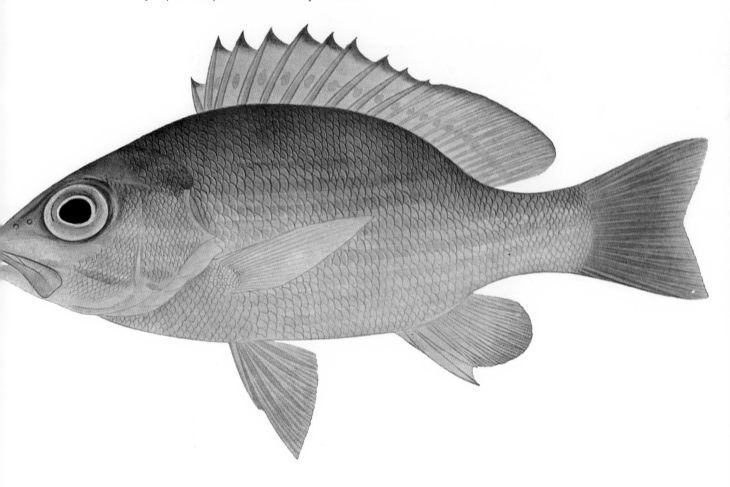

308. *Lutjanus superbus* (Castelnau). A native of Australia, this species may prove to be synonymous with *L. bohar*. Illustration by Kumada.

309.   *Lutjanus fulviflamma* (Forskal). Another coastal species entering brackish water of estuaries and mangrove areas, as well as occurring on reefs. Photo by Dr. Shih-chieh Shen. Ma-Kung, Pescadore Islands. (216 mm standard length)

310. *Lutjanus lineolatus* (Ruppell). The gold-striped snapper attains a length of about 15 inches. Note the yellow stripes following the oblique scale rows above the lateral line. Photo by Dr. Shih-chieh Shen. Taiwan. (138 mm standard length)

311. *Lutjanus fulviflamma* (Forskal). Dark color phase. Widespread species of the Indo-Pacific region. To over a foot in length. Photo by Dr. Shih-chieh Shen. Taiwan. (96 mm standard length)

312. *Lutjanus fulviflamma* (Forskal). Light phase. Snappers are hardy and survive well in captivity but are predators and will make short work of smaller fishes in an aquarium. Photo by Dr. Shih-chieh Shen. Taiwan. (120 mm standard length)

1288

313.
Lutjanus fulviflamma
(Forskal). Young. The
lateral yellow stripes are
not well developed at
this stage. The dark
stripes present may be
remnants of a juvenile
pattern. Photo by Dr.
Shih-chieh Shen.
Taiwan. (66.5 mm
standard length)

314.
Lutjanus vitta (Quoy and
Gaimard). Indo-Pacific.
This species retains the
dark lateral band at all
ages. Photo by Dr.
Shih-chieh Shen.
Taiwan. (90 mm
standard length)

315.
Lutjanus vitta (Quoy and
Gaimard). This species
grows to a length of
about 14 inches. Photo
by Dr. Shih-chieh Shen.
Taiwan. (145 mm
standard length)

316. Unidentified grunt (family Pomadasyidae). This is possibly a species of *Parapristipoma*, as it roughly fits the description of *P. trilineatum*, which occurs around Taiwan. Photo by Dr. Shih-chieh Shen. Tang-Shui, northern part of Taiwan. (250 mm standard length)

317. Unidentified snapper (family Lutjanidae), of the genus *Lutjanus*. Photo by Dr. Shih-chieh Shen. Tang-Shui, northern part of Taiwan. (325 mm standard length).

318. *Pristipomoides argyrogrammicus* (Valenciennes). Distributed from southern Japan to Africa. Illustration by Kuma-da.

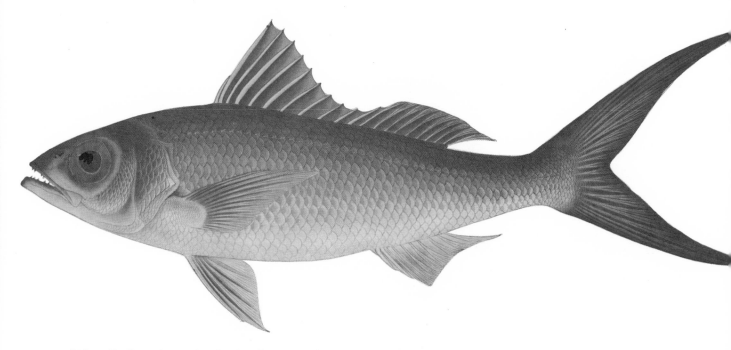

319. *Etelis carbunculus* Cuvier. Recorded from the Hawaiian Islands to Africa and the Atlantic. Illustration by Kumada.

320. *Pristipomoides filamentosus* (Cuvier and Valenciennes). A rather deep water fish reaching a length of up to one meter. Illustration by Arita.

321. *Aprion virescens* Cuvier and Valenciennes. Mostly Pacific Ocean but does extend to India. Rare. Reaches a length of about 350 mm. Illustration by Arita.

322. *Aphareus rutilans* Cuvier and Valenciennes. Widespread Indo-Pacific species from the Hawaiian Islands to the Red Sea. Illustration by Arita.

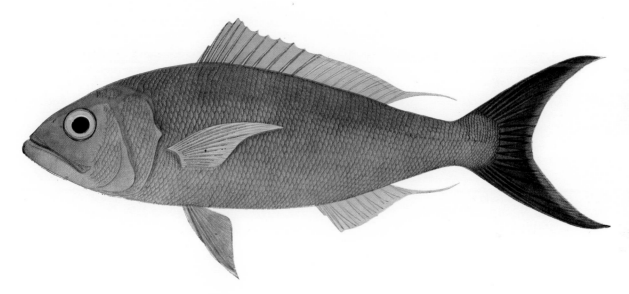

323. *Nemipterus virgatus* (Houttuyn). A good food fish that attains a length of about 500 mm. Spawns from May to August in Japanese waters. Photo by Dr. Shih-chieh Shen. Taiwan. (231.8 mm standard length)

324. *Nemipterus bathybus* Snyder. Note the yellow abdominal stripe in this species. It is absent in the closely related *N. virgatus*. Photo by Dr. Shih-chieh Shen. Ma-Kung, Pescadore Islands. (152.4 mm standard length)

325. *Caesio xanthonotus* Bleeker. Indo-Pacific species. Reaches a length of about 8 inches. Illustration by Arita.

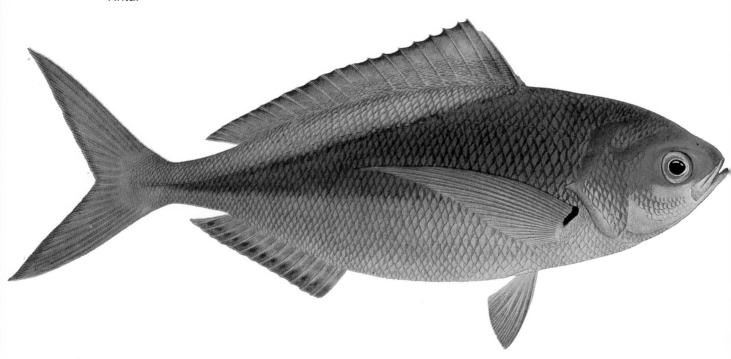

326. *Pterocaesio tile* (Cuvier and Valenciennes). Indo-Pacific. Grows to a size of about one foot. Photo by Dr. Shih-chieh Shen. Hing-Chuen, southern tip of Taiwan. (218 mm standard length)

327. *Caesio caerulaureus* (Lacepede). This species is found in schools near coral reefs. Photo by Dr. Shih-chieh Shen. Taiwan. (186 mm standard length)

328. *Pterocaesio diagramma* (Bleeker). Indo-Pacific. Attains a length of about 10 inches. Photo by Dr. Shih-chieh Shen. Taiwan. (160 mm standard length)

329. *Pterocaesio diagramma* (Bleeker). Note the color change between this individual and the one above. Photo by Dr. Shih-chieh Shen. Taiwan. (58 mm standard length)

330. *Lethrinus miniatus* (Bloch and Schneider). This species has also been called *Lethrinella miniata*. Reaches a length of just over 2½ feet. Can undergo color pattern changes as shown. Illustrations by Tomita and Arita.

331. *Lethrinus fletus* Whitley. Normally a coral reef fish with the young moving into mangrove areas. Photo by Dr. Shih-chieh Shen. Tan-Shui, northern tip of Taiwan. (134.4 mm standard length)

332. *Lethrinus fletus* Whitley. Lighter phase. The throat in this species is red in color. Photo by Dr. Shih-chieh Shen. Ma-Kung, Pescadore Islands. (158.6 mm standard length)

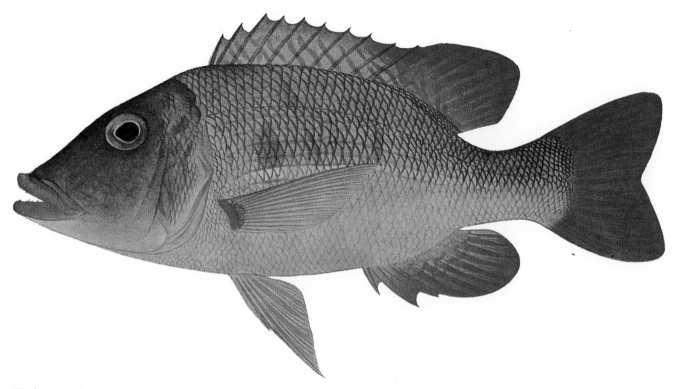

333. *Lethrinus kallopterus* Bleeker. The grayish spot between the lateral line and pectoral fin is blackish in juveniles. Illustration by Tomita. Indo-Pacific.

334. *Lethrinus leutjanus* (Lacepede). Coral reefs. The head may become purplish brown and there may be dusky bars on its back. Illustration by Kumada.

335. *Lethrinus variegatus* (Valenciennes). Also called *Lethrinella variegata*. Indo-Pacific. Deeper water. Illustration by Tomita.

336. *Lethrinus xanthocheilus* Klunzinger. This Indian Ocean (including the Red Sea) species probably does not reach Taiwan. Illustration by Arita.

337. *Lethrinus harak* (Forskal). Indo-Pacific. Attains a length of about 1½ feet. Illustration by Arita.

338. *Gymnocranius microdon* (Bleeker). Species of this genus are rarely imported for the aquarium trade. Illustration by Tomita.

339. *Gymnocranius griseus* (Temminck and Schlegel). Western Pacific to Africa. Rather common in deeper waters. Illustration by Kumada. (to 360 mm)

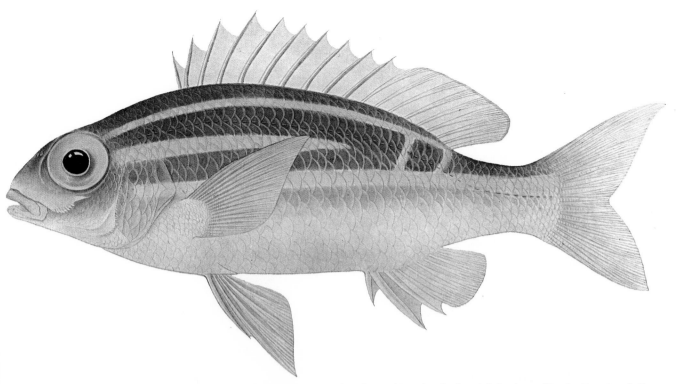

340.   *Scolopsis cancellatus* (Cuvier). Hawaii to India. Attains a length of about 9 inches. Illustration by Arita.

341.   *Nemipterus ovenii* (Bleeker). Practically nothing has been reported on the adaptability of species of *Nemipterus* to the aquarium. Illustration by Arita.

342.   *Scolopsis monogramma* (Cuvier). The yellow bar from eye to eye across the interorbital space is one of the differentiating characters of this species. Photo by Dr. Shih-chieh Shen. Ma-Kung, Pescadore Islands. (175.6 mm standard length)

343. *Scolopsis monogramma* (Cuvier). Adult. This species reaches a length of over one foot. Photo by Dr. Shih-chieh Shen. Tang-Shui, northern part of Taiwan. (236 mm standard length)

344. *Scolopsis monogramma* (Cuvier). Should feed well on crustaceans or fish flesh in captivity. Photo by Dr. Shih-chieh Shen. Peng-Hu, an island offshore from Taiwan. (157.4 mm standard length)

345. *Scolopsis vosmeri* (Bloch). Widespread in the tropical waters of the Indo-Pacific. Photo by Dr. Shih-chieh Shen. Ma-Kung, Pescadore Islands. (152.0 mm standard length)

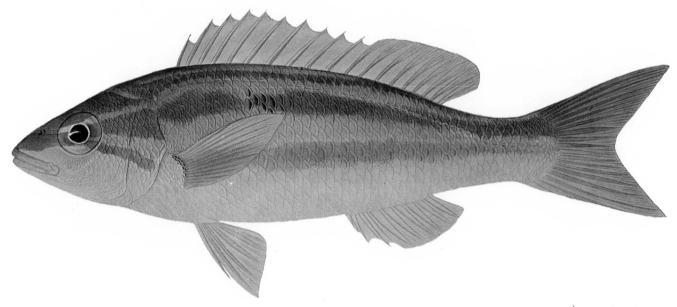

346. *Pentapodus caninus* (Cuvier). A shallow water species not quite reaching a foot in length. Illustration by Arita.

347. *Scolopsis vosmeri* (Bloch). Reaches a length of about 10 inches. Illustration by Arita.

348. *Scolopsis bilineatus* (Bloch). One of the most distinctive species of scolopsids. Grows to about 8 inches in length. Photo by Dr. Shih-chieh Shen. Taiwan. (161 mm standard length)

349. *Scolopsis cancellatus* (Cuvier). The whitish or yellow cross bars are not present in this individual. Photo by Dr. Shih-chieh Shen. (110 mm standard length)

350. *Scolopsis cancellatus* (Cuvier). Part of the light cross-banding has appeared. Note also the black spot in the anterior part of the dorsal fin. Photo by Dr. Shih-chieh Shen. (113.2 mm standard length)

351. *Hapalogenys nigripinnis* (Temminck and Schlegel). Known only from Japan and Korea to south China. Note the papillae on the chin. Illustration by Tomita.

352. *Hapalogenys mucronatus* (Eydoux and Souleyet). Similar distribution as *H. nigripinnis*. Illustration by Arita.

353. *Pomadasys hasta* (Bloch). This grunt (family Pomadasyidae) attains a length of about 1½ feet. Photo by Dr. Shih-chieh Shen. Taiwan. (197.6 mm standard length)

354. *Pomadasys maculatus* (Bloch). A shallow water species which may enter the brackish waters of bays and estuaries. Photo by Dr. Shih-chieh Shen. Taiwan. (102 mm standard length)

355. *Pomadasys maculatus* (Bloch). Reaches the size of about 18 inches. Photo by Dr. Shih-chieh Shen. Taiwan. (114.4 mm standard length)

356. *Argyrops spinifer* (Forskal). Distributed from Japan to Australia and across the Indian Ocean to the Red Sea. Illustration by Tomita.

357. *Evynnis japonica* Tanaka. Only reported from Japan and Korea to south China. Inhabits deeper waters. Spawning season is late in the year, from September to December. Illustration by Tomita.

358. *Evynnis cardinalis* (Lacepede). Similar to the above but has the third and fourth spines elongate and filamentous. Photo by Dr. Shih-chieh Shen. Ma-Kung, Pescadore Islands. (181.0 mm standard length)

359. *Rhabdosargus sarba* (Forskal). Common inshore fish which spawns in the early spring in Japan. Size to 400 mm. Illustration by Arita.

360. *Acanthopagrus berda* (Forskal). Common in shallow coastal waters and entering river mouths. To 2½ feet in length. Photo by Dr. Shih-chieh Shen. Houng-La-Tsuen, southern tip of Taiwan. (103.6 mm standard length)

361. *Gymnocranius griseus* (Temminck and Schlegel). Note how closely this species of penta-
podid resembles the sparids on this page. Photo by Dr. Shih-chieh Shen. Taiwan. (180 mm
standard length)

362. *Evynnis japonica* Tanaka. One of the main food fishes of Japan, reaching a size of about 400 mm. Photo by
Dr. Shih-chieh Shen. Ma-Kung, Pescadore Islands. (225 mm standard length)

363. *Chrysophrys auratus* (Bloch and Schneider). The young of this Australian species is much like that of its close relative *C. major* (see PMF Book 2, p. 434). Illustration by Kumada.

364. *Pelates quadrilineatus* (Bloch). The trumpeter perch is common in bays and near river mouths where they enter brackish water. Illustration by Tomita.

365. *Pelates quadrilineatus* (Bloch). Here the humeral spot is very faded and the dorsal fin spot smaller. Photo by Dr. Shih-chieh Shen. Ma-Kung, Pescadore Islands. (105.0 mm standard length)

366. *Therapon jarbua* (Forskal). The crescent perch is found in the brackish waters of bays and estuaries. Photo by Dr. Shih-chieh Shen. Taiwan. (105 mm standard length)

367. *Therapon jarbua* (Forskal). This species attains a length of about 10 inches. Photo by Dr. Shih-chieh Shen. Taiwan. (94.5 mm standard length)

368. *Therapon theraps* Cuvier. Also sometimes referred to as *Eutherapon theraps*. Also marine and brackish waters of bays and estuaries. Illustration by Tomita.

Family SCIAENIDAE
CROAKERS AND DRUMS

This large family of fishes contains species which range from a few inches to the very large *Johnius* species reaching a length of 6 feet and a weight of 100 pounds. Larger yet is the tutuava of the East Pacific, *Cynoscion macdonaldi*, which may weigh in at over 200 pounds.

The croakers are found around the world in tropical and temperate waters, with most species inhabiting the warmer waters. They are coastal fishes conspicuously absent from the Pacific Islands. One theory is that they need estuarine waters, which are absent or scarce in the smaller islands, as a habitat for their young. It has been noted that certain Caribbean species have also adapted to the insular, reef-type environment. The sciaenids in general occur over sandy areas in shallow water and freely enter the low salinity areas of estuaries. Some species are completely adapted to fresh water in South America.

Croakers are good sport fishes, putting up a decent fight when hooked. Wherever they are found, they are usually used for food, their flesh being good, even delicious in some cases. There are a few species that are not edible, and some of the larger fishes become less palatable or tasteless with size. They are carnivorous, voraciously chasing some of their co-inhabitants of the estuarine waters such as herring and mullet.

Probably one of the more interesting aspects of these fishes is the production of sound. They certainly earn their common names of croakers and drums. The sounds are so loud they can be heard by the occupants of a boat which is in the area of these fishes. The sounds are produced by means of a combination of muscles and swim bladder. The movement of muscles attached to the swim bladder causes the sound, which is amplified as it resonates in the chamber of the bladder. The reason for the sounds is not clearly known, although it has been found that the sounds increase during the spawning season and also vary from day to night. The muscles producing the sound are apparently controlled by the fish and the sound therefore is under voluntary control. The large air bladders are used by man in the production of a poor grade of isinglass. Some species of sciaenids lack the swim bladder but still make sounds by grinding their teeth.

The family Sciaenidae contains an estimated 160 species, making it one of the larger families of fishes. The body is oblong to elongate and slightly compressed. The dorsal fin is deeply notched and barely connected at the base, giving the appearance of having two dorsal fins. The spiny portion may, in some species, be folded back into a groove. The anal fin of sciaenids has one or two anal spines, never three as is common to many other bony fishes. The anal fin itself has a much shorter base than the dorsal fin. The body and bases of the vertical fins are covered with thin, adherent scales. Unlike most other fishes, the lateral line does not stop at the base of the caudal fin but continues onto the fin itself. The mouth is large, ventral, terminal, oblique, or horizontal, and provided with bands of villiform teeth, the outer and inner rows often enlarged. The palate is toothless. There may be some barbels on the chin or they may be absent; when present, barbels may be single or in several rows. The superficial bones of the head are often provided with muciferous pores, most often on the chin or snout. Among the other special developments of the croakers are the enlarged earbones or otoliths.

Probably the most important sciaenids, as far as aquarists are concerned, are the members of genus *Equetus* of the Atlantic, which includes the high-hats, etc.

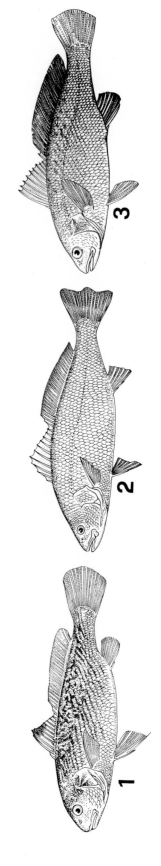

369. *Nibea mitsukurii* (Jordan and Snyder). Known only from southern Japan, Korea and China. Closely related to (1) *Argyrosomus nibe*, (2) *A. japonicus*, and (3) *Nibea albiflora*. Illustrations by Arita.

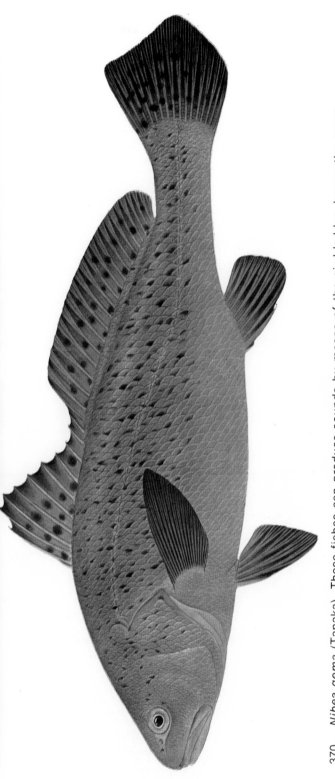

370. *Nibea goma* (Tanaka). These fishes can produce sounds by means of the air bladder, hence the name croakers. Illustration by Arita.

371. *Argyrosomus argentatus* (Houttuyn). Also known under the genus *Otholithes*. Inhabits deeper water, but young appear in bays and other shallow areas. Japan, Korea, and China. Illustration by Tomita.

372. *Rachycentron canadum* (Linnaeus). The cobia is a well known game fish. Apparently circumtropical, occurring in the Pacific, Indian and Atlantic Oceans. Illustration by Arita.

Family RACHYCENTRIDAE
COBIA

A single genus and species, *Rachycentron canadum*, makes up this family. It is a large streamlined fish reaching a length of over six feet and a weight of 150 pounds or more. It inhabits the tropical and subtropical waters of the world (although it may be absent from the eastern Pacific).

The body is elongate, the head broad and flattened. The mouth is terminal, wide, and provided with villiform teeth. Additional teeth may be found on the tongue and palate (vomer and palatine bones). The eyes are small and provided with a small adipose eyelid. The soft dorsal and anal fins are similarly shaped and composed of 25-35 rays and 20-28 rays, respectively. The spinous dorsal fin is not easily visible and is formed by about eight very short free spines. The caudal fin is lunate in the adults but quite different in the juveniles. The juveniles have the inner caudal fin rays prolonged and, with maturity, the proportions of the tail change to form a squarish or slightly emarginate caudal in sub-adults and eventually the lunate tail of the adult.

The cobia is easily identifiable by the broad dark horizontal stripes on its sides. The young cobia resemble closely the young of some remoras or sharksuckers, and this has led to many interesting speculations on the relationships and evolution of these fishes.

Although reaching a large size, cobia do well in captivity. They need large tanks of course and might be seen in the large circular tanks of public aquaria. It is primarily a piscivore but will eat crustaceans without hesitation. In some areas it has even been called the crab-eater. Other common names attached to this fish are the sergeant-fish, black kingfish, bonito, etc., as well as some interesting non-English names such as gabur laut, buntut karbo, dalag dagat, moan-tchoan, tchoan-yue, etc.

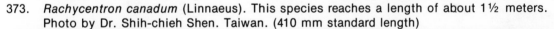

373. *Rachycentron canadum* (Linnaeus). This species reaches a length of about 1½ meters. Photo by Dr. Shih-chieh Shen. Taiwan. (410 mm standard length)

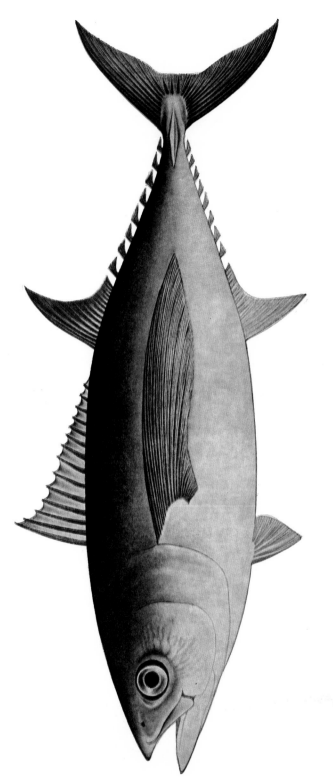

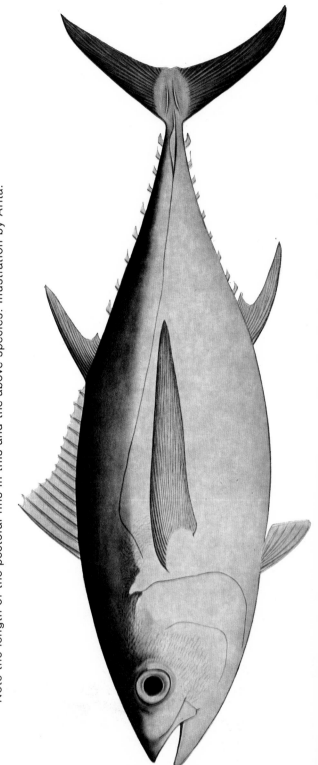

374. *Thunnus alalunga* (Bonnaterre). Also known as *Germo alalunga*. Known from almost all tropical waters. Reaches a length of about one meter. Illustration by Tomita.

375. *Thunnus obesus* (Lowe). Also known as *Parathunnus obesus*. Circumtropical. Reaches a length of about 2 meters. Note the length of the pectoral fins in this and the above species. Illustration by Arita.

Family SCOMBRIDAE
TUNAS AND MACKERELS

The tunas and mackerels are streamlined fishes of the pelagic or open waters of the world. They inhabit the surface waters though some may also be found in deeper waters, depending upon temperature and/or food supply. They travel in small to very large schools, and the migration patterns of some of the species are fairly well known.

Some of the tunas are among the largest of the true fishes, the bluefin (*Thunnus thynnus*) being reported to attain a length of 14 feet and a weight of almost a ton. Both tunas and mackerel are of great economic importance—canned tuna can be found in just about every supermarket —and are highly respected game fishes. Tuna tournaments are always a source of excitement to anglers.

The typical tuna or mackerel is very streamlined. It has a spindle-shaped body tapering back to a slender caudal peduncle. On each side of the caudal peduncle are keels, generally a central large one flanked by two smaller ones, although the true mackerels (*Scomber* and allies) usually have only the two smaller keels. The dorsal and anal fins are followed by a series of small detached finlets. The scalation is usually reduced to minute, closely adherent scales, somewhat heavier in the shoulder region and there forming what is called the corselet, or may be absent entirely. There are often grooves in the body of the fish so that the fins, when folded back or held close to the body, provide very little drag. Also in connection with streamlining, the head is sharply pointed. The mouth is large and the jaws are provided with strong, sharp teeth, those of the tunas conical and little flattened, those of the Spanish mackerels triangular and flattened.

Tunas have been kept in captivity both for experimental purposes and exhibition. Most success has been attributed to placing them in round or oval tanks with plenty of room. The reason for the rounded tanks is to allow these fishes to swim continuously in one direction without meeting an obstruction. They are predators and easily fed on fish, squid, or other animal matter.

376. *Euthynnus affinis* (Cantor). Spawns in the early spring (about May) at Taiwan. Reaches one meter in length. Photo by Dr. Shih-chieh Shen. Ma-Kung, Pescadore Islands.

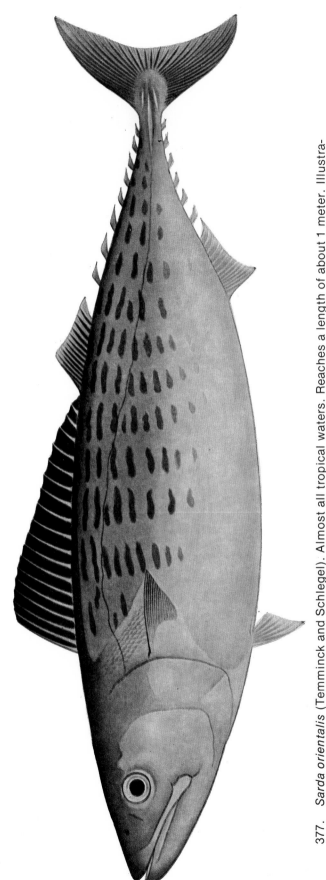

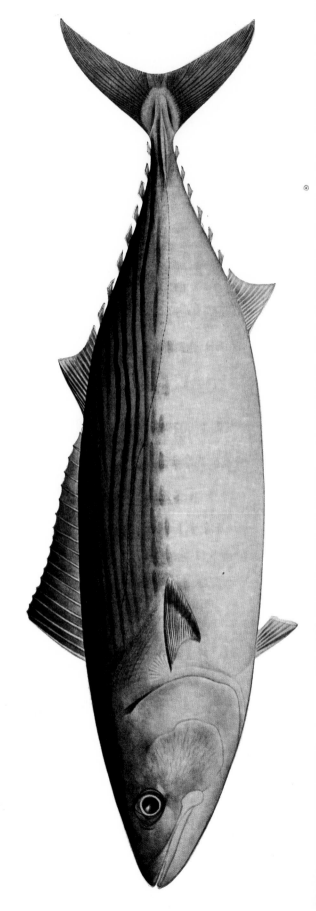

377. *Sarda orientalis* (Temminck and Schlegel). Almost all tropical waters. Reaches a length of about 1 meter. Illustrations by Arita. (Young above, adult below.)

378. *Scomber japonicus* Houttuyn. Also known under the name *Pneumatophorus japonicus*. An important food fish. Known from California to the east coast of Africa. Photo by Dr. Shih-chieh Shen. Taiwan. (173 mm standard length)

379. *Euthynnus pelamis* (Linnaeus). Commonly known as skipjack, bonito, or watermelon. A very important food fish from almost all warm seas. Photo by Dr. Shih-chieh Shen. Taiwan. (284 mm standard length)

380. *Euthynnus affinis* (Cantor). Known from Japan and Korea to China, and from Hawaii. Photo by Dr. Shih-chieh Shen. Taiwan. (260.4 mm standard length)

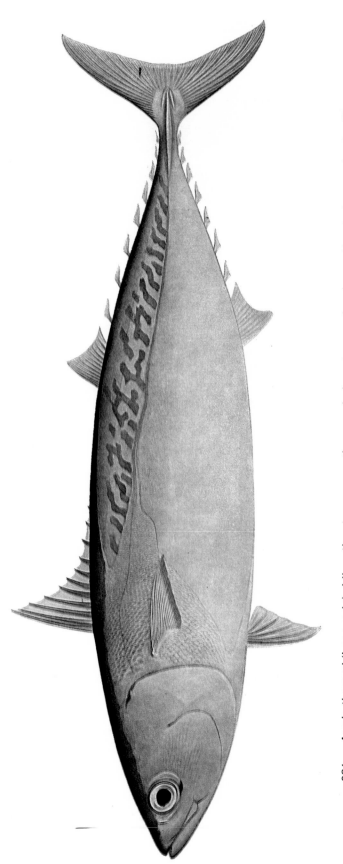

381.   *Auxis thazard* (Lacepede). Like other tunas, mostly oceanic in nature and congregating in large schools. Illustration by Arita.

382.   *Scomberomorus niphonius* (Cuvier). Known from Japan to Australia. Its closest relatives are (1) *S. sinensis*, (2) *S. koreanus*, and (3) *S. commerson*. Illustrations by Tomita.

383. Young tuna, probably *Euthynnus pelamis* (Linnaeus). Although small tuna may be collected and placed in aquaria, they rarely do well. Photo by Dr. Shih-chieh Shen. Taiwan. (81 mm standard length)

384. *Thunnus thynnus* (Linnaeus). Popularly called the bluefin tuna. An excellent food fish found in most temperate and tropical waters. Illustration by Tomita. (to 3 meters)

385. *Calliurichthys japonicus* (Houttuyn). Range extends from Japan and Korea to Australia and across the Indian Ocean to India. Illustration by Arita.

386. *Synchiropus* sp. Probably related to *S. stellatus* of the Indian Ocean or *S. ocellatus* of the western Pacific. Photo by Dr. Shih-chieh Shen. (61.5 mm standard length)

387. *Synchiropus lineolatus* (Valenciennes). Distinctive are the rows of black-edged blue spots in the anal fin and the red of the mouth. Photo by Dr. Shih-chieh Shen. Taiwan. (64.6 mm standard length)

388. *Synchiropus* sp. The dark phase. This species has been referred to as *Synchiropus lili*, but that seems unlikely. *S. lili* might even be a synonym of *S. ocellatus*. Photo by K.H. Choo. Taiwan.

389. *Petroscirtes breviceps* (Bleeker). The young of this species may be a mimic of *Meiacanthus grammistes*. Photo by Dr. Shih-chieh Shen. Houng-Lo-Tsiun, southern tip of Taiwan. (104.4 mm standard length)

390. *Aspidontus taeniatus* Quoy and Gaimard. This is the blenny that mimics the cleaner wrasse, *Labroides dimidiatus*. Photo by K.H. Choo. Taiwan.

391. *Springeratus xanthosoma* (Bleeker). One of the two clinids from the China Sea area. The other species, *Clinus nematopterus*, does not have the elevated anterior dorsal spines. A livebearer. Photo by Dr. Shih-chieh Shen. Taiwan. (59 mm standard length)

392. *Springeratus xanthosoma* (Bleeker). The genus was named for Dr. Victor G. Springer by Dr. Shih-chieh Shen. Photo by Dr. Shih-chieh Shen. Taiwan. (top to bottom: 71.8, 71.6, and 49.8 mm standard length)

393. *Meiacanthus grammistes* (Valenciennes). This blenny attains a length of about 3 inches. Photo by Dr. Shih-chieh Shen. Taiwan. (73.4 mm standard length)

394. *Meiacanthus grammistes* (Valenciennes). Usually found in shallow water. Occasionally imported for marine aquarists. Photo by K.H. Choo.

395.
Ecsenius lineatus.
The distinctive color
pattern makes this
species relatively
easy to identify.
Photo by Dr. Shih-
chieh Shen. Taiwan.
(54.6 mm standard
length)

396.
Salarias fasciatus
(Bloch). This blenny
attains a length of
about 4 inches.
Found in inshore
pools and shallows.
Photo by Dr. Shih -
chieh Shen. Taiwan.
(99 mm standard
length)

397.
Cirripectes sp.
Blennies are easily
caught in tidal pools
or very shallow water
and make hardy aqua-
rium inhabitants.
Photo by Dr. Shih-
chieh Shen. Taiwan.
(72.3 mm standard
length)

398. *Istiblennius* ? Our blenny expert says this might not be *Istiblennius* but genus *Praealticus*. This points up the extreme difficulty of trying to identify fishes without recourse to the specimens. Photo by Dr. Shih-chieh Shen. Taiwan. (45 mm standard length)

399. *Cirripectes* sp. Note the row of cirri across the back of the head just anterior to the dorsal fin. This and head cirri are useful in identification. Photo by Dr. Shih-chieh Shen. (56.1 mm standard length)

400.
Istiblennius lineatus
(Valenciennes). Male.
Also called *Salarias
lineatus* or *Halma-
blennius lineatus*.
Grows to over 6
inches. Photo by Dr.
Shih-chieh Shen.
Taiwan. (88.5 mm
standard length)

401.
Istiblennius lineatus
(Valenciennes).
Normally found in
very shallow waters
and tidal pools. Photo
by Dr. Shih-chieh
Shen. Taiwan. (86
mm standard length)

402.
Istiblennius lineatus
(Valenciennes).
Female. Males have a
well developed crest
on top of their head
as seen in photo
number 400. Photo by
Dr. Shih-chieh Shen.
Taiwan. (88 mm
standard length)

403. *Istiblennius edentulus* (Bloch and Schneider). Male. Found in shallow waters and tidal pools subject to strong wave action. Grows to a length of more than 6 inches. Photo by Dr. Shih-chieh Shen. Taiwan. (93 mm standard length)

404. *Istiblennius edentulus* (Bloch and Schneider). Male. Known in some areas as the smooth-lipped blenny. Photo by Dr. Shih-chieh Shen. Taiwan. (58.5 mm standard length)

405. *Istiblennius meleagris* (Valenciennes). Female. Attains a length of about 5 inches. Shallow waters and tidal pools. Photo by Dr. Shih-chieh Shen. Taiwan. (88.5 mm standard length)

406. *Balistoides niger* (Bonnaterre). The jaws of this fish are very strong and can cause a bit of damage if used on a person. Photo by Dr. Shih-chieh Shen. Chi-Lung, northeastern part of Taiwan. (121.4 mm standard length)

407.   *Balistoides niger* (Bonnaterre). Note the faded white spots in the upper part of the fish. Only small individuals have this. No one has even seen or photographed one under 8 cm. Photo by K.H. Choo. Taiwan.

408.   *Balistoides niger* (Bonnaterre). This clown triggerfish has spread his fins as a defensive gesture. Photo by K.H. Choo. Taiwan.

409.
Balistes flavimarginatus (Ruppell). Juvenile. Widespread throughout the tropical Indo-Pacific. Photo by Dr. Shih-chieh Shen. Taiwan. (60.5 mm standard length)

410.   *Balistoides niger* (Bonnaterre). Occurs from the Red Sea to Mexico but apparently not found in quantity. Highly prized as an aquarium fish. This is the smallest specimen ever photographed. Photo by Dr. Shih-chieh Shen. Chi-Lung, northeastern part of Taiwan. (121.4 mm standard length)

411. *Balistoides flavimarginatus* (Ruppell)? This individual seems to combine characteristics of *B. flavimarginatus* and *Balistes viridescens*. Photo by K.H. Choo. Taiwan.

412. *Pseudobalistes fuscus* (Bloch and Schneider). One of the more colorful juveniles for the marine aquarium. Photo by K.H. Choo. Taiwan.

413.   *Odonus niger* (Ruppell). Red-toothed triggerfish. Attains a length of about 20 inches. Illustration by Tomita.

414.   *Abalistes stellaris* (Lacepede). The starry triggerfish attains a length of about 2 feet. Illustration by Arita.

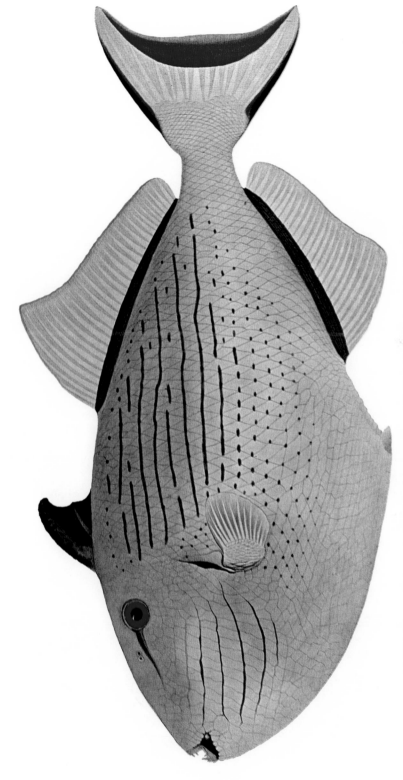

415. *Xanthichthys ringens* (Linnaeus). Sargassum triggerfish. Young are occasionally captured near sargassum weed. Circumtropical. Illustration by Kumada.

416. *Rhinecanthus aculeatus* (Linnaeus). The Humuhumu (its Hawaiian name) is one of the more popular of aquarium triggerfishes. It reaches a length of about 1 foot. Photo by K.H. Choo. Taiwan.

417. *Rhinecanthus aculeatus* (Linnaeus). This species occurs from Hawaii to the African coast. Photo by Dr. Shihchieh Shen. Yuan-Shan, southern tip of Taiwan. (157 mm standard length)

418. *Rhinecanthus rectangulus* (Schneider). Tropical waters of the Indo-Pacific. Attains a length of 200 mm. Photo by K.H. Choo. Taiwan.

419. *Rhinecanthus rectangulus* (Schneider). Triggerfishes can often be "tamed." They will learn to eat food from their owners fingers. Photo by Dr. Shih-chieh Shen. Yuan-Shan, southern tip of Taiwan. (84.4 mm standard length)

420.
*Cantherhines
dumerili* (Hollard).
Filefish normally have
a single enlarged
dorsal spine
compared to three for
the triggerfishes.
Photo by K.H. Choo.
Taiwan.

421. *Rhinecanthus
verrucosus* (Lin-
naeus). Indo-Pacific.
Reaches a length of
about 9 inches. Photo
by Dr. Shih-chieh
Shen. Taiwan. (47
mm standard length)

422. *Canthidermis
maculatus* (Bloch).
Circumtropical.
Mostly an offshore
fish. Juveniles occa-
sionally are available
in marine aquarium
fish stores. Photo by
Dr. Shih-chieh Shen.
Taiwan. (205 mm
standard length)

423. *Balistapus undulatus* (Mungo Park). Indo-Pacific in distribution. Reaches a length of about 30 cm. Photo by Dr. Shih-chieh Shen. Taiwan. (152 mm standard length)

424. *Balistapus undulatus* (Mungo Park). The lateral stripes may fork to form several branches as this individual shows. Photo by K.H. Choo. Taiwan.

425. *Amanses scopas* (Cuvier). The spines on the side of this fish are characteristic of this species. Photo by Dr. Shih-chieh Shen. Taiwan. (154.5 mm standard length)

426. *Amanses scopas* (Cuvier). Males have longer, bristle-like spines; females have shorter, more erect brush-like spines. Photo by Dr. Shih-chieh Shen. Taiwan. (143.6 mm standard length)

Family MONACANTHIDAE
FILEFISHES

The filefishes are a small to moderate sized group of fishes that inhabit the coastal waters of tropical and temperate areas. Rather than use of speed for fleeing a pursuing predator, the filefishes depend to a great extent on camouflage or protective coloration and their physical make-up. Most have subdued colors which make them inconspicuous in their natural habitat. Others have fringes or flaps of skin which enhance their resemblance to sea grasses and algae such as sargassum, which they frequently use for shelter. As for their physical attributes, they have a long dorsal fin spine that can be erected and locked into place like the triggerfishes. They also have a tough, finely spiney, leathery skin which is difficult to penetrate. This last characteristic has earned them the common names of filefish, leatherjackets, and sandpaper fish.

Filefishes are compressed fishes with very small scales usually provided with one or more small spines. The caudal peduncle may be armed with additional elongate spines as extra protection. The acanthurids (surgeonfishes) have been considered to be related to plectognaths (which includes the filefishes), a theory that gains and loses favor from time to time. Perhaps the propensity for armature on the caudal peduncle may have something to do with this relationship. There are two dorsal fins, the first consisting of the previously mentioned elongate spine and a smaller second spine for locking the first. The soft dorsal and anal fins are alike and opposite in position. The caudal fin is rounded to truncate, and the ventral fins are absent. The pelvic bones have coalesced and project through the body wall. A small movable or immovable spine may be present, and the pelvic bones support a flap of skin which may be small or greatly expandable.

427. *Amanses scopas* (Cuvier). The dorsal fin spine is in the retracted position here. If danger threatens the spine will be raised. Photo by K.H. Choo. Taiwan.

428.
Navodon modestus
(Gunther). Known from
Japan to Africa. Also
known under the name
Amanses modestus.
Illustration by Tomita.

429.   *Chaetodermis spinosissimus* (Quoy and Gaimard). The starry-shaped objects covering this fish are modified
scales, hence the common name prickly leatherjacket. Illustration by Tomita.

430. *Paraluteres prionurus* (Bleeker). This filefish does not get much larger than 3 or 4 inches. Indo-Pacific in distribution. Photo by K.H. Choo. Taiwan.

431. *Pervagor melanocephalus* (Bleeker). The caudal fin of this species is quite colorful. One common name for this fish is the lace-finned leatherjacket. Photo by K.H. Choo. Taiwan.

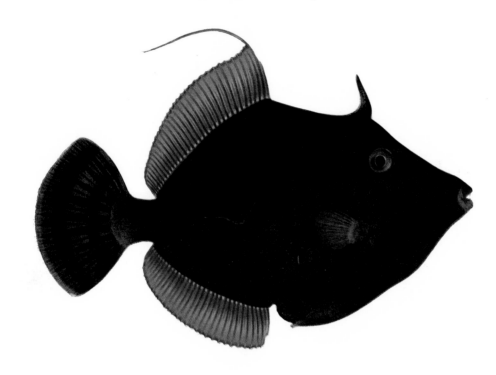

432.
Stephanolepis cirrhifer (Temminck and Schlegel). Commonly found near shore among floating weeds. Korea and the East China Sea. Illustration by Arita. (to 300 mm)

433.   *Cantherhines sandwichensis* (Quoy and Gaimard). Circumtropical in distribution. Attains a length of about 15 inches. Photo by Dr. Shih-chieh Shen. Wan-Li-Tung, southern tip of Taiwan. (124.6 mm standard length)

434. *Monacanthus filicauda* Gunther. Thread-tailed filefish. May also be referred to under the name *Arotrolepis fili-cauda*. Illustration by Tomita.

435. *Cantherhines sandwichensis* (Quoy and Gaimard). Often called the wire-netting filefish. Males have two pairs of barbs on sides of caudal peduncle. Photo by Dr. Shih-chieh Shen. Huing-Tsai-Kuing, southern tip of Tai-wan. (110.4 mm standard length)

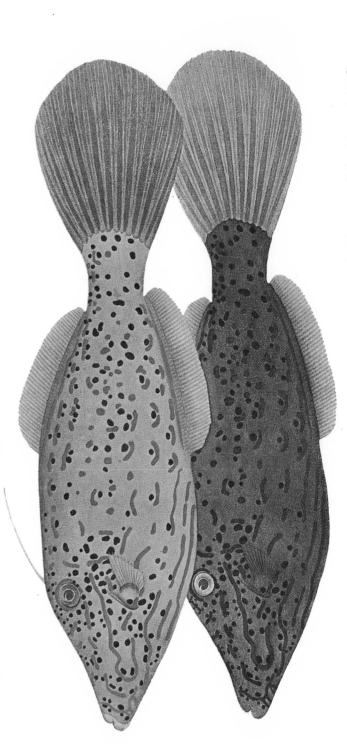

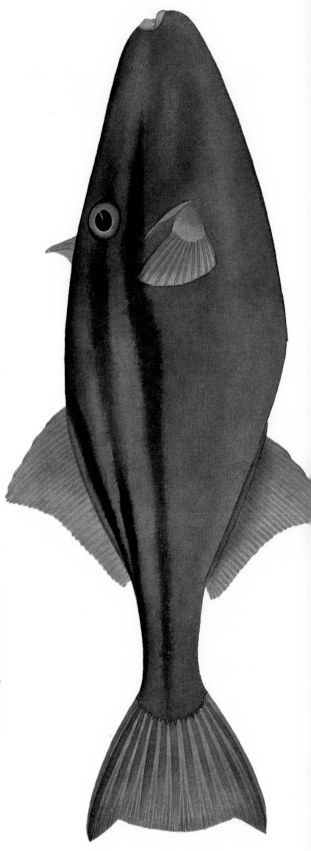

436. *Aluterus scriptus* (Forster). The scrawled or scribbled filefish may go under the name *Osbeckia scripta*. Circumtropical. Illustration of two color phases by Arita.

437. *Navodon ayraud* (Quoy and Gaimard). Chinaman's filefish. This species has also been placed in the genera *Cantherhines*, *Pseudomonacanthus*, and *Nelusetta*. Illustration by Tomita.

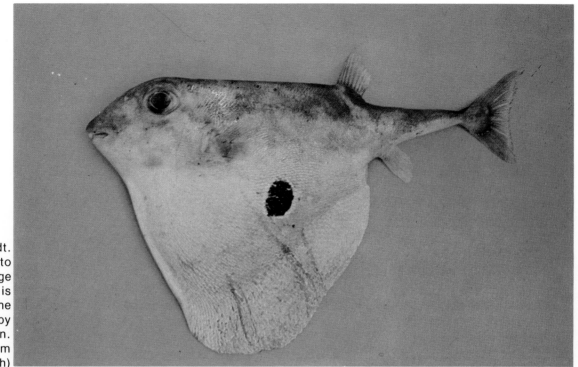

438. *Triodon bursarius* Reinhardt. Known from Japan to Africa. The large ventral flap is supported by the pelvic bone. Photo by Dr. Shih-chieh Shen. Taiwan. (224.4 mm standard length)

439. *Arothron stellatus* (Bloch). A large puffer (to about 3 feet) which is also capable of inflating its body. Photo by Dr. Shih-chieh Shen. Ma-Kung, Pescadore Islands. (228 mm standard length)

440. *Chaetodermis spinosissimus* (Quoy and Gaimard). The skin flaps aid in the camouflage of this fish when it is hiding among the seaweeds. Photo by K.H. Choo. Taiwan.

441. *Canthigaster valentini* (Bleeker). The small sharp-nosed puffers often swim with their fins folded like this. Locomotion is provided mainly by their dorsal and anal fins. Photo by K.H. Choo. Taiwan.

442 & 443. *Canthigaster cinctus* (Richardson) (above) and *C. valentini* (Bleeker) (below) resemble each other in the barring across the back but differ in many other color and pattern features. Photos by Dr. Shih-chieh Shen. *Canthigaster cinctus* from Pai-Sha, southern tip of Taiwan (57.2 mm standard length); *C. valentini* from Nanwan, southern tip of Taiwan. (61 mm standard length)

444. *Canthigaster bennetti* (Bleeker). A small puffer attaining a length of about 2 inches. Photo by K.H. Choo. Taiwan.

445. *Canthigaster bennetti* (Bleeker). The radiating lines from the eye are common to several species of sharpnosed puffers. Photo by Dr. Shih-chieh Shen. Pai-Sha, southern tip of Taiwan. (57.2 mm standard length)

446. *Canthigaster janthinopterus* (Bleeker). An Indo-Pacific species that grows to a length of about 3 inches. Photo by Dr. Shih-chieh Shen. Wan-Li-Tung, southern tip of Taiwan. (55.8 mm standard length)

447. *Canthigaster janthinopterus* (Bleeker). Note the pattern of lines on the head and at the base of the dorsal fin. Photo by K.H. Choo. Taiwan.

448.
Ostracion cubicus
Linnaeus. Juvenile.
Small boxfishes such
as these make excel-
lent aquarium inhabi-
tants. They are some-
times picked on by
larger fishes,
however. Photo by Dr.
Shih-chieh Shen.
Taiwan. (21.0 mm
standard length)

449. *Ostracion cubicus* Linnaeus. Juvenile. Newly hatched brine shrimp will usually help keep this fish alive and well. A varied diet is recommended. Photo by K.H. Choo. Taiwan.

450.   *Aracana aurita* (Shaw). This is one cowfish that would command a high price. The male has a dark stripe in the caudal fin. This bizarre species is from relatively deep water in Australia. Illustration by Kumada.

451.
Lactoria cornuta
(Linnaeus). Known
from Hawaii to the
Red Sea. Attains a
length of 20 inches.
Photo by Dr. Shih-
chieh Shen. Taiwan.
(178.4 mm standard
length)

452.   *Ostracion meleagris* Shaw. Female. The juveniles are similar to the females, but the adult males are brightly
colored with blue and orange markings. Photo by Dr. Shih-chieh Shen. Wan-Li-Tung, southern tip of Taiwan.

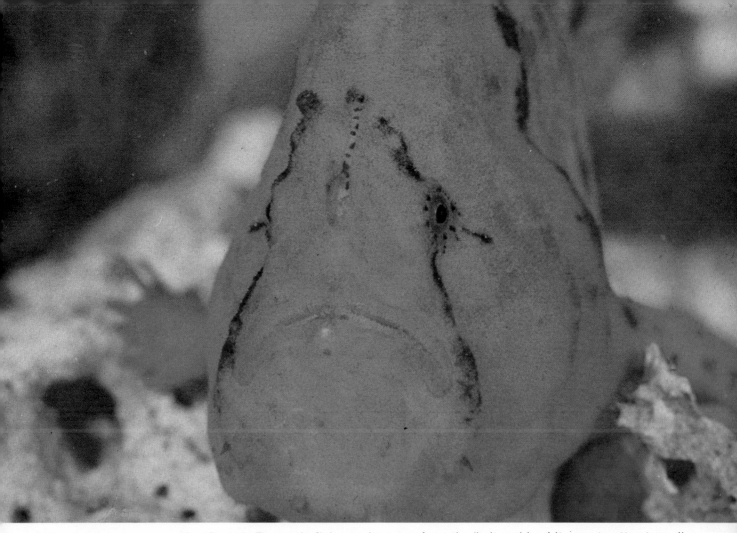

453. *Antennarius nummifer* (Cuvier). The anglerfish gets its name from the 'bait and lure' it uses to attract small fishes. It is a modified dorsal fin ray. Photo by K.H. Choo. Taiwan.

454. *Antennarius nummifer* (Cuvier). The ocellated spot at the dorsal fin base helps identify this fish. Photo by K.H. Choo. Taiwan.

455.
Histrio histrio
(Linnaeus). Its
habitat is a clump of
sargassum weed,
which it resembles
very closely. Photo by
Dr. Shih-chieh Shen.
Taiwan.

456. *Histrio histrio* (Linnaeus). The modified pectoral and pelvic fins enable this fish to "walk" among the branches of the sargassum. Photo by Dr. Shih-chieh Shen. Pai-Sha, southern tip of Taiwan. (82.4 mm stan-standard length)

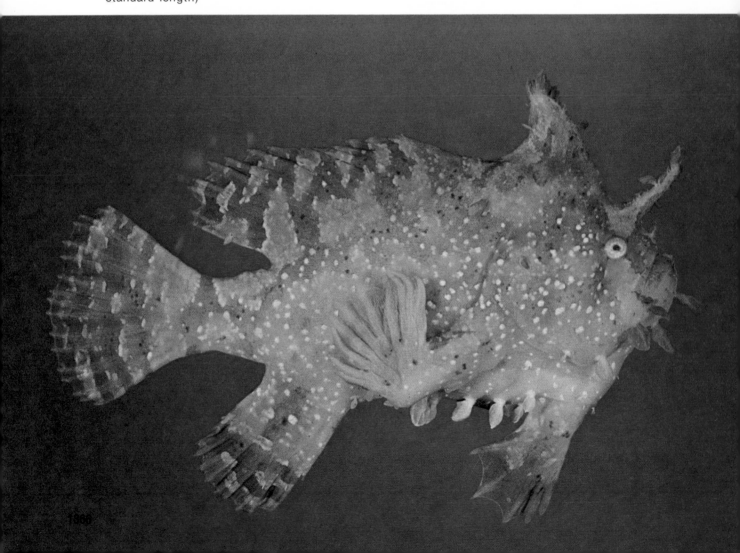

Index

Page numbers in **bold** face refer to illustrations

The following index contains entries for subject matter and illustrations contained in this book and its companion volumes, *Pacific Marine Fishes*, 1-4. Some of the names used in earlier volumes of this series, however, have been revised to reflect an updated or otherwise changed nomenclatural standing; all such names listed in text and index of these volumes are listed in this index but are referenced to show the revised identifications.

A

Abalistes stellaris, **395, 1344**
Ablennes anastomella, **332**
Ablennes hians, **924, 926**
Abudefduf, 701
Abudefduf affinis, **1025**
Abudefduf amabilis, **304**
Abudefduf annulatus, **738**
Abudefduf aureus, **305**
Abudefduf aureus, **196**
  (See Chromis analis)
Abudefduf behnii, **200, 206, 1036**
Abudefduf bengalensis, **194**
Abudefduf biocellatus, **204, 732, 733**
Abudefduf bitaeniatus, **206**
  (See Abudefduf behnii)
Abudefduf curacao, **1023**
Abudefduf cyaneus, **190, 192, 193,
  197, 203, 302, 1036**
Abudefduf dickii, **730, 1028**
Abudefduf dickii, **201**
  (See Abudefduf johnstonianus)
Abudefduf flavipinnis, **1037**
Abudefduf glaucus, **734, 1033**
Abudefduf johnstonianus, **201**
Abudefduf lacrymatus, **207, 731,
  735, 1029**
Abudefduf leucogaster, **200, 304**
Abudefduf leucopomus, **1032, 1035**
Abudefduf leucozona, **307, 1034,
  1035**
Abudefduf melanopus, **203, 306,
  307, 1034**
Abudefduf oxyodon, **206**
Abudefduf parasema, **303**
Abudefduf parasema, **203**
  (See Abudefduf cyaneus)
Abudefduf phoenixensis, **307**
Abudefduf rex, **202, 1031**
Abudefduf saxatilis, **195, 1023,
  1024, 1025**
Abudefduf septemfasciatus, **1023**
Abudefduf sexfasciatus, **195, 736,
  1024**
Abudefduf sordidus, **194, 306, 727,
  728, 729**
Abudefduf sparoides, **737**
Abudefduf thoracotaeniatus, **195**
Abudefduf uniocellata, **190, 192, 197**
  (See Abudefduf cyaneus)
Abudefduf vaigiensis, **737**
Abudefduf xanthonotus, **203**
  (See Abudefduf melanopus)
Abudefduf xanthurus, **200**
  (See Abudefduf behnii)
Abudefduf sp., **201**
  (See Pomacentrus dorsalis)
Abudefduf sp., **200**
  (See Abudefduf leucogaster)
Acanthocepola, 931
Acanthocepola indica, **930, 931**
Acanthogobius flavimanus, **179**

Acanthopagrus berda, **1314**
ACANTHURIDAE, 84, 793
Acanthurus, 803
Acanthurus bleekeri, **384**
Acanthurus chronixis, **796**
Acanthurus dussumieri, **385**
Acanthurus gahhm, **382, 795**
Acanthurus glaucopareius, 91, **386**
Acanthurus guttatus, **384**
Acanthurus japonicus, **91, 386**
Acanthurus leucosternon, 85, **381,
  797**
Acanthurus lineatus, 85, 90, **387,
  1148, 1149**
Acanthurus nigrofuscus, 86
Acanthurus olivaceous, 86, **383**
Acanthurus pyroferus, 89
Acanthurus tennenti, **795**
Acanthurus triostegus, 90, **792, 793**
Acanthurus sp., **794**
Acentrogobius cauerensis, **635**
Acentrogobius hoshinonis, **178**
Acentrogobius ornatus, **1014**
Acentrogobius sp., **1014**
Adioryx, 230, 231, 689
Adioryx andamanensis, **691**
Adioryx caudimaculatus, **339, 691**
Adioryx diadema, 234, **1061**
Adioryx lacteoguttatus, **339, 693,
  1063**
Adioryx microstomus, **339**
Adioryx rubra, 235, **1062**
Adioryx spinifer, **234, 689, 690, 692**
Adioryx spinosissimus, **1061**
Adioryx tiere, **341**
Adioryx xantherythrus, 230, **340**
Adioryx sp., **1061**
Aeoliscus, 319
Aeoliscus strigatus, **320, 321**
Aesopia, 1099
Aesopia heterorhinos, **1099**
Aetobatus narinari, **1076**
Aetomylaeus, 1077
African clown wrasse, 578
African squirrelfish, 235
Aholeholes, 236, 308
Albula vulpes, **1043**
Alectis ciliaris, **1050**
Alectis indica, 426, **1050**
Alectis major, **1051**
ALEPISAURIDAE, 1257
Alepisaurus borealis, **1256**
Alepisaurus ferox, **1257**
Alfoncino, 548, 1161
Allard's clownfish, 705
Alutera monoceros, **125**
Alutera scripta, **122, 1356**
ALUTERIDAE, 819
Amanses scopas, **1350, 1351**
AMARSIPIDAE, 1220
Amblyapistus taenianotus, **517, 962**
Amblycirrhitus, 155, 660
Amblycirrhitus bimacula, **1142**

Amblygobius albimaculatus, **634,
  635**
Amora, 219
Amphiprion, 181, **287**
Amphiprion akindynos, 288, **292**
Amphiprion allardi, 701, **705, 708**
Amphiprion biaculeatus, **190, 301**
Amphiprion chrysopterus, **191, 296,
  297, 1019**
Amphiprion clarkii, **180, 183, 185,
  292, 704, 708, 709, 714, 715, 1018,
  1019**
Amphiprion ephippium, **292**
Amphiprion frenatus, **184, 186, 187,
  1020, 1021**
Amphiprion latezonatus, **289**
Amphiprion laticlavius, **183**
Amphiprion melanopus, **293**
Amphiprion nigripes, **561, 710-14**
Amphiprion ocellaris, **188, 189, 298,
  299, 300, 301, 1021**
Amphiprion percula, **188**
Amphiprion perideraion, **182, 185,
  294, 295, 1017**
Amphiprion polymnus, **183**
Amphiprion sandaracinos, **188**
Amphiprion tricinctus, **290, 291**
Amphiprion xanthurus, **180**
Amphiprion sp., **706, 707**
Anago anago, **352**
Anampses caeruleopunctatus, **144,
  145, 440, 623**
Anampses cuvieri, **445**
Anampses meleagrides, **442, 864**
Anampses neoguinaicus, **863**
Anampses rubrocaudatus, **440**
  (= Anampses chrysocephalus)
Anampses twistii, **440, 863**
Anampses sp., **142**
  (See Anampses neoguinaicus)
Anemonefishes, 181, 289, 701
Angelfishes, 7, 39, 781
Angel sharks, **1069**
Anglerfish, 509
Anglerfishes, 258
Anguilla, 260
Anguilla japonica, **351**
ANTENNARIIDAE, 258
Antennarius biocellatus, **828**
Antennarius chironectes, **529**
Antennarius coccineus, **529**
Antennarius hispidus, **528**
Antennarius indicus, **529**
Antennarius nox, 259
Antennarius nummifer, **528, 1365**
Antennarius phymatodes, **530**
Antennarius sanguifluus, 259
Antennarius tridens, 259, **270, 532**
Antennarius sp., **528**
Anthias, 643
Anthias squammipinnis, **489, 490,
  649, 1224**
Anthias sp., **646, 742, 760**

1369